HURLYBURLY

Other Plays by David Rabe

HURLYBURLY

DAVID RABE

GROVE WEIDENFELD

New York

Published by Grove Weidenfeld
A division of Grove Press, Inc.
841 Broadway
New York, NY 10003-4793

Library of Congress Cataloging-in-Publication Data

Rabe, David.
    Hurlyburly / David Rabe.
    p.   cm.
    ISBN 0-8021-3251-0 (alk. paper) : $8.95
    I. Title.
    [PS3568.A23H8   1991]
    812'.54—dc20   90-25816
                                          CIP

Manufactured in the United States of America

Printed on acid-free paper

Designed by Irving Perkins Associates

First Evergreen Edition 1985

Revised Evergreen Edition 1991

1   3   5   7   9   10   8   6   4   2

For Ellen Neuwald

Hurlyburly was produced at the Westwood Playhouse in Los Angeles, Barbara Ligeti, Randy Finch, William P. Suter, Steven Ullman, Willette Klausner and The Landmark Entertainment Group, producers, on November 16, 1988, with the following cast:

EDDIE	Sean Penn
PHIL	Danny Aiello
MICKEY	Scott Plank
ARTIE	Michael Lerner
DONNA	Jill Schoelen
DARLENE	Belinda Bauer
BONNIE	Mare Winningham

Directed by DAVID RABE

Scenery and lighting were by Richard Meyer; costumes by Marianna Elliot; sound by John Gottlieb; production stage manager was Frank Marino.

Hurlyburly was originally produced at the Goodman Theatre, Chicago, Gregory Mosher, Artistic Director, on April 2, 1984, with the following cast:

EDDIE	William Hurt
PHIL	Harvey Keitel
MICKEY	Christopher Walken
ARTIE	Jerry Stiller
DONNA	Cynthia Nixon
DARLENE	Sigourney Weaver
BONNIE	Judith Ivey

Directed by MIKE NICHOLS

The scenery was by Tony Walton; costumes by Ann Roth; lighting by Jennifer Tipton; sound by Michael Schweppe. The production stage manager was Peter Lawrence.

The New York premiere of the play took place on June 21, 1984, at the Promenade Theatre, presented by Icarus Productions and Frederick M. Zollo, with Ivan Bloch and ERB Productions and William P. Suter as Associate Producer. It opened with the same cast and designers as in Chicago and under the direction of Mike Nichols.

Hurlyburly premiered on Broadway in New York at the Ethel Barrymore Theatre on August 7, 1984, again presented by Icarus Productions and Frederick M. Zollo, with Ivan Bloch and ERB Productions and William P. Suter as Associate Producer. The cast and designers were the same as in the two previous presentations, except that the part of MICKEY was played by Ron Silver instead of Christopher Walken, and the sound was by Otts Munderloh. The direction was again by Mike Nichols.

CHARACTERS

Eddie   Darlene

Phil   Bonnie

Mickey   Donna

Artie

ACT ONE

SCENE 1

Time: Morning a little while ago.

Place: A two-story house crowded into one of the canyons between Sunset Boulevard and Mulholland Drive in the Hollywood Hills.

A somewhat spacious living room leading into an open kitchen makes up the entire first floor of the house. Steps lead upstairs to an exposed balcony which overlooks the living room. A rail runs along the balcony and stairway. Three doors feed onto the balcony. The doors lead into EDDIE's bedroom, which is stage right, and MICKEY's bedroom, which is a little right of the top of the stairway. Between them is the bathroom. Stage right there is a couch and a low coffee table. On top of it are scripts, photos, résumés, newspapers and magazines, their disarray flowing onto the couch and the floor around it. At the stage right end of the couch is an end table and to the right of it a television atop a stand. There is room to walk between the TV and the end table. The TV faces toward the couch and an armchair, which is slightly downstage of the couch and slightly left of center. The chair is large, comfortable and on a swivel so it can turn toward the TV and the couch, or it can swing full front or swing to stage left and face the direction of the kitchen. Near the chair is a hassock. On the hassock is a box, 8 inches by 6 inches by 3 inches. The box is itself a miniature of a mummy or the lid is decorated by a model of a mummy. Directly upstage of the couch and yet slightly off center is the door to the outside. Along the back wall and at a slight angle is a door to a closet on the outside of which is a coat rack. Adjacent to the front door and on the stage left side is a window seat, the outdoor foliage visible in the window above it. Bookcases fill the walls to the stage right of the door, both the upstage side and the stage right wall. At the downstage edge of the stage right bookcases is a record player with records. Pillows lie on the floor beside it. Atop the record player is a large dictionary. Support beams of the second floor run down creating an upstage area focused around the door and distinct from the couch or living room area. The kitchen is an L-shaped counter running downstage on the stage right side and then in the stage left direction. There are four swivel chairs on the outside of the L and one on the inside. Upstage are the stove, refrigerator, cabinets. There is a phone on the nook counter; it is situated on the downstage leg, the far stage left end. To facilitate certain moves, the phone should probably be mobile, wireless. A waste can is located by this same end of the L. The nook itself has shelves facing front and back in which there are liquor bottles, magazines, scripts, résumés. Scripts, résumés lie all over the upstage bookshelves also. Two or three scripts lie in a pile on the landing of the stairway. The floor of the living room and the stairs are carpeted; the kitchen is linoleum.

The house is completely surrounded by wild vegetation, which is visible through greenhouse-like windows in the living room and kitchen. At the sides of the stage, the vegetation forms a border, bleeding into the interior of the house. It is worth noting that in the characters' speeches, phrases such as "watchamacallit," "thing-

amajig," "blah-blah-blah" and "rapateta" abound.
*These are phrases used by the characters to keep them-
selves talking and should be said unhesitatingly with
the authority and conviction with which one would
have in fact said the missing word. In general, the play
should proceed without pauses between speeches or
words. There is no need to race, but there is little room
for pauses.*

In the Willie Nelson album Stardust, *referred to in the
first scene, there is a harmonica riff about halfway
through "Unchained Melody." A two-minute loop of
this refrain should be made to be used as the theme.
This theme starts the show. As the curtain rises,* EDDIE *is
asleep on the couch in an isolated pool of light. The
harmonica riff, quite wistful, begins in the darkness
building quickly until it is quite loud, as the lights
come up to discover* EDDIE, *sleeping on the couch. He is a
mess, his shirt out, wrinkled, unbuttoned, his trousers
remaining on him only because one leg is yet tangled
around one ankle. When* EDDIE *is clearly established for
a couple beats the sound of the TV begins to enter into
the music. The music and the sound of the TV fight and
the lights are coming up throughout the house as the TV
sound erodes and then banishes the music and* PHIL
*comes in the door. The TV plays, the music is gone, the
lights are up as* PHIL, *a muscular, anxious man in a
hurry, comes rushing in. He wears sunglasses and a dark
sport coat over a pullover shirt, and he carries the morning L.A. paper and rushes straight up to the sleeping*
EDDIE, *grabbing* EDDIE *by the foot to wake him up. It is
worth noting that* EDDIE *subtly adopts* PHIL's *manner-
isms when alone with him.*

PHIL: Eddie!

EDDIE (*startled, sitting up*): What? (*As* PHIL *tosses the newspaper onto* EDDIE's *lap.*)

PHIL: Eddie, you awake or not?

EDDIE (*disoriented, he bolts to his feet and stands there*): I don't know. How about you?

PHIL (*taking off his sunglasses, sticking them in his jacket pocket*): Eddie, I'm standin' here. How you doin'?

EDDIE: I don't know. Did I leave the door open?

PHIL: It was open.

EDDIE (*a man in command, almost bragging, he staggers to the door, shutting it, and then comes wandering back toward the couch, carrying the newspaper with him, dragging his trousers along behind him*): I come home last night, I was feelin' depressed. I sat around, I watched some TV. Somebody called and hung up when I answered. I smoked some dope, took a couple of ludes. The TV got to look very good. It was a bunch of shit, but it looked very good due to the dope and due to the ludes. (*Dropping the newspaper on the end table beside the couch, he turns off the TV using the remote control and sags onto the couch.*) So I musta fell asleep at some point. (*He is sinking back as if he might go back to sleep.*)

PHIL (*poking* EDDIE *again to make sure he wakes up,* PHIL *heads for the kitchen, as* EDDIE *sits back up*): Maybe I'll make us some coffee. Where is everything? By the stove and stuff?

EDDIE (*sitting back up*): What time is it?

PHIL: It's over.

EDDIE: What?

PHIL: Everything.

EDDIE (*rising, staggering toward the kitchen, his trousers dragging along by the ankle, he is a little irritated that* PHIL *is bothering him in this way*): What EVERY-THING?

PHIL: Me and Susie.

EDDIE: Whata you mean, "everything"? (*At the sink,* EDDIE *soaks a towel.*)

PHIL: Everything. The whole thing. You know. Our relationship. I really fucked up this time. I really did. (PHIL *rattles the tea kettle to find that there is water in it, then sets it on the stove, which he turns on.*)

EDDIE: You had a fight. So what? Give her a little time and call her up, you know that. Don't be so goddamn negative.

PHIL: This was a big one.

EDDIE: Bigger than the last one?

PHIL: Yeah.

EDDIE: So what'd you do, shoot her? (*He starts away toward the living room. Silence, as* PHIL *is preparing the instant coffee in the cups.* EDDIE *freezes, whirls back.*) You didn't shoot her, Phil. You got a gun?

PHIL: On me? (*Patting his jacket pockets, he pulls out a silver, chrome-plated snub-nosed .38.*)

EDDIE: You didn't shoot her, Phil.

PHIL: No.

EDDIE (*he heads back toward the couch, taking his towel and a bottle of aspirin with him*): So, she'll take you back. She always takes you back.

PHIL: I went too far. She ain't going to take me back.

EDDIE: You want me to call her?

PHIL: She'll give you the fucking business. She hates you.

EDDIE (*irritated that* PHIL *should even say such a thing*): What are you talking about, she hates me? Susie don't hate me. She likes me.

PHIL: She hates you. She tol' me. In the middle of the fight.

EDDIE (*his head killing him, he takes some aspirin*): What are you talking about: you two are in the middle of this bloodbath—the goddamn climactic go-round of your three-year career in, you know what I mean, marital carnage and somewhere in the peak of this mother-fucker she takes time out to tell you she hates good ol' Eddie. Am I supposed to believe that?

PHIL (*as* PHIL, *bringing a can of beer, joins* EDDIE *on the couch*): I was surprised, too. I thought she liked you.

EDDIE: You're serious.

PHIL: Yeah.

EDDIE: Fuck her—what a whore! She acted like she liked me.

PHIL: I thought she liked me.

EDDIE: I thought she liked you, too. I mean, she don't like anybody, is that the situation, the pathetic bitch? (*Leaping to his feet, he heads for the stairway to the second floor, kicking off his trousers as he goes.*)

PHIL: I knew she hated Artie.

EDDIE: I knew she hated Artie, too. But Artie's an obnoxious, anal-obsessive pain in the ass who could make his best friend hire crazed, unhappy people with criminal tendencies to cut off his legs, which we have both personally threatened to do. So that proves nothing. (*As he is about to enter the bathroom, he pauses to look down at* PHIL.) I mean, what the hell does she think gives her justification to hate me?

PHIL (*he drifts toward the base of the stairs, looking up*): She didn't say.

EDDIE (*he freezes where he stands*): She didn't say?

PHIL: No.

EDDIE (*bolting into the bathroom, he yells on from within it*): I mean, did she have a point of reference, some sort of reference from within your blowup out of which she made some goddamn association which was for her justification that she come veering off to dump all this unbelievable vituperative horseshit over me—whatever it was. I wanna get it straight. (*Toilet is flushed within the bathroom.*)

PHIL: You got some weed? I need some weed. (*On the base of the stairs, as* EDDIE *emerges from the bathroom, pulling on a pair of raggedy, cut-off gym pants as he heads down the stairs.*)

EDDIE: So what'd she say about me? You know, think back. So the two of you are hurling insults and she's a bitch, blah-blah-blah, you're a bastard, rapateta. (*Picking up the dope box from the hassock, he is about to go to the couch.*) So in the midst of this TUMULT where do I come in?

PHIL: You're just like me, she says.

EDDIE: What? (*He stops; can't believe it.*) We're alike? She said that?

PHIL: Yeah—we were both whatever it was she was calling me at the time.

EDDIE (*flopping down on the arm of the chair, he hands* PHIL *a joint*): I mean, that's sad. She's sad. They're all sad. They're all fucking pathetic. What is she thinking about?

PHIL: I don't know.

EDDIE: What do you think she's thinking about?

PHIL: We're friends. You know. So she thinks we got somethin' in common. It's logical.

EDDIE: But we're friends on the basis of what, Phil? On the basis of opposites, right? We're totally dissimilar is the basis of our friendship, right?

PHIL: Of course. (*As the tea kettle whistles,* PHIL *heads for the kitchen,* EDDIE *following.*)

EDDIE: I mean, I been her friend longer than I been yours. What does she think, that I've been—what? More sympathetic to you than her in these goddamn disputes you

two have? If that's what she thought she should have had
the guts to tell me, confront me! (*Having dug a second
joint from the dope box, he heads back for the couch
now, leaving the box on the counter, as* PHIL *pours the
hot water into the coffee cups and stirs them.*)

PHIL: I don't think that's what she thought.

EDDIE: SO WHAT WAS IT?

PHIL: I don't know. I don't think she thinks.

EDDIE: None of them think, I don't know what they do.

PHIL: They don't think. (*Carrying the two cups, he heads for
the couch and* EDDIE.)

EDDIE: They express their feelings. I mean, my feelings are
hurt, too.

PHIL: Mine, too.

EDDIE: This is terrible on a certain level. I mean, I liked you
two together.

PHIL: I know. Me, too. A lot of people did. I'm very upset. Let
me have some more weed. (*Reaching back he grabs the
joint from* EDDIE.) It was terrible. It was somethin'. Blah-
blah-blah!

EDDIE: Rapateta. Hey, absolutely. (*Sagging back onto the
couch, lying back to rest, the towel on his forehead.*)

PHIL: Blah-blah-blah! You know, I come home in the middle a
the night—she was out initially with her girlfriends, so
naturally I was alone and went out, too. So I come home,
I'm ripped, I was on a tear, but I'm harmless, except I'm

on a talking jag, you know, who cares? She could have some sympathy for the fact that I'm ripped, she could take that into consideration, let me run my mouth a little, I'll fall asleep, where's the problem? That's what you would do for me, right?

EDDIE: Yeah.

PHIL: She can't do that.

EDDIE: What's she do? What the hell's the matter with her, she can't do that?

PHIL (rising, a little agitated, he takes off his coat, tosses it onto the armchair, pacing a little): I'm on a tear, see, I got a theory how to take Las Vegas and turn it upside down like it's a little rich kid and shake all the money out of its pockets, right?

EDDIE: Yeah. So what was it?

PHIL: It was bullshit, Eddie. (Sitting back down opposite EDDIE.) I was demented and totally ranting, so to that extent she was right to pay me no attention, seriously, but she should of faked it. But she not only sleeps, she snores. So I gotta wake her up, because, you know, the most important thing to me is that, in addition to this Las Vegas scam, I have this theory on the Far East, you know; it's a kind of vision of Global Politics, how to effect a real actual balance of power. She keeps interrupting me. You know, I'm losing my train of thought every time she interrupts me. It's a complex fucking idea, so I'm asking her to just have some consideration until I get the whole thing expressed, then she wants to have a counterattack, I couldn't be more ready.

EDDIE: She won't do that?

PHIL: No.

EDDIE: That's totally uncalled for, Phil. All you're asking for is civilization, right? You talk and she talks. That's civilization, right? You take turns!

PHIL: I don't think I'm asking for anything unusual, but I don't get it.

EDDIE: Perverse.

PHIL: Perverse is what she wrote the book on it. I am finally going totally crazy. (*Jumping back up on his feet.*) I've totally lost track of my ideas. I'm like lookin' into this hole in which was my ideas. I arrive thinkin' I can take Vegas and save the world. Forty-five seconds with her and I don't know what I'm talking about. So I tell her— "LISTEN!—lemme think a second, I gotta pick up the threads." She says some totally irrelevant but degrading shit about my idea and starts some nitpicking with which she obviously intends to undermine my whole fucking Far Eastern theory on the balance of powers, and I'm sayin', "Wait a minute," but she won't. So WHACK! I whack her one in the face. Down she goes.

EDDIE: You whacked her.

PHIL: I whacked her good. You see my hand. (*Moving away from* EDDIE, PHIL *holds his hand out behind him.*)

EDDIE (*leaning forward a little to look at* PHIL*'s hand*): You did that to your hand?

PHIL: Her fuckin' tooth, see.

EDDIE: You were having this political discussion with which she disagreed, so you whacked her out, is that right?

PHIL: (*he flops down on the hassock, smoking the dope*): It wasn't the politics. I didn't say it was the politics.

EDDIE: What was it? (*Moving to* PHIL, EDDIE *hands* PHIL *his coffee.*)

PHIL: I don't know. I had this idea and then it was gone.

EDDIE: Yeah. (*Pacing behind* PHIL, *thinking, seeming to almost interrogate him.*)

PHIL: It was just this disgusting cloud like fucking with me and I went crazy.

EDDIE: Right. Whata you mean?

PHIL: You know this fog, and I was in it and it was talking to me with her face on it. Right in front of me was like this cloud with her face on it, but it wasn't just her, but this cloud saying all these mean things about my ideas and everything about me, so I was like shit and this cloud knew it. That was when it happened.

EDDIE: You whacked her.

PHIL: Yeah.

EDDIE: Was she all right?

PHIL: She was scared, and I was scared. I don't know if I was yelling I would kill her or she was yelling she was going to kill me.

EDDIE: Somebody was threatening somebody, though.

PHIL: Definitely.

EDDIE (*settling down on the edge of the armchair behind* PHIL, EDDIE *puts his arm around* PHIL): So try and remember. Was it before you whacked her or after you whacked her that she made her reference to me?

PHIL: You mean that she hated you?

EDDIE: Yeah.

PHIL: Before. It was in the vicinity of Vegas, I think, but it gets blurry.

EDDIE (*thoughtfully returning to the couch: he has his answer now*): So what musta happened is she decided I had some connection to your Vegas scam and this was for her justification to dump all this back-stabbing hostility all over me.

PHIL: She didn't say that. She just says we're both assholes.

EDDIE: But it would be logical that if this petty, cheap-shot animosity was in the vicinity of Vegas, it would have to do with Vegas. THAT WOULD ONLY BE LOGICAL.

PHIL: EXCEPT THAT SHE AIN'T LOGICAL. (*He is headed to join* EDDIE, *who seems to have gotten things wrong.*)

EDDIE: True.

PHIL (*sitting down on the couch*): SHE'S JUST A NASTY BITCH AND I MARRIED HER.

EDDIE: You know what I think?

PHIL: What?

EDDIE: She hates men.

Phil: Whata you mean?

Eddie: She hates you, she hates me. She hates men. I don't know what else to think. It's a goddamn syllogism. Susie hates Phil, Susie hates Eddie.

Phil: And Artie, too.

Eddie: Artie, Eddie, Phil are men, she hates men. The fucker's irrefutable, except that's not how it works, GODDAMNIT. (*Angrily grabbing his glasses from the coffee table, he heads to the dictionary lying atop the record player.*)

Phil: What?

Eddie: You go from the general to the particular. I'm talking about a syllogism, here.

Phil: Yeah.

Eddie (*irritated, he paces behind the couch, leafing through the dictionary*): Damnit! What the hell goes the other way?

Phil: Which way?

Eddie: Something goes the other goddamn way!

Phil: What?

Eddie (*pacing back and forth, he comes around the couch*): You start from the particular in something. Susie hates Eddie, Susie hates Phil. Phil and Eddie are men, therefore, blah-blah-blah . . . Oh, my God, do you know what it is? (*Sitting on the couch.*)

PHIL: What?

EDDIE: Science! What goes the other way is science, in which you see all the shit like data and go from it to the law. (*Slamming shut the dictionary, he sets it on the end table, his glasses on top of it.*) This is even better. We have just verified, and I mean scientifically, the bitch has been proven to basically hate all men. She doesn't need a reason to hate me in particular—she already hates me in the fucking abstract. (*Upstairs, the toilet flushes and* EDDIE *stands, looking up at the bathroom.*)

PHIL: You gonna call her?

EDDIE: You want me to? I will if you want me to. (*He is rushing up the stairs.*)

PHIL: You said you were gonna!

EDDIE: That was before I understood the situation. Now that I understand the situation, the hell with her. The bitch wants to go around hating me in the fucking abstract! Are you nuts? Call her? (*Having reached the bathroom door, he pounds on it. He pounds and pounds.*) I wouldn't piss on her if the flames were about to engulf her goddamn, you know, central nervous system! (*As* MICKEY *staggers out of the bathroom onto the balcony heading to reach into his own room and grab a robe from off the door.*)

MICKEY: Didn't I beg you to let me have some goddamn quiet this morning? Eddie, I begged you!

EDDIE: Phil has left Susie again, only this time it's final!

MICKEY: So what are YOU screaming about?

Phil (*starting up the stairs*): The deceitful bitch has been bad-mouthing Eddie. That's been part of the problem from the beginning.

Eddie (*as* Mickey *heads down the stairs,* Eddie *follows him*): I mean, she thinks she can do this shit and get away with it? He goes back, he's nuts. He deserves her. You go back this time, Phil, I'm never gonna speak to you again.

Phil: (*backing down the stairs,* Mickey *between himself and* Eddie): I know that. I agree with you.

Mickey: He's not serious, Phil.

Eddie: Whata you know about it? (*Poking* Mickey *from behind.*)

Mickey: You're serious, if Phil goes back to his wife, you don't ever want to speak to him again?

Eddie (*as* Mickey *turns and heads to the kitchen,* Eddie *is face to face with* Phil, *and he puts his finger in* Phil's *face to tell him*): I'm serious. (*And then he races after* Mickey *with* Phil *following.*)

Phil: I hate her anyway!

Eddie: See!

Mickey: That's not serious.

Eddie: Says you! I know when I'm serious and I'm serious, and Phil knows it even if you don't.

Phil: I'm done with her!

Eddie: See! (*Grabbing a vial of coke from the box atop the counter,* EDDIE *heads off for the couch,* PHIL *following him.*)

MICKEY: You guys are in a fucking frenzy here. Have some breakfast, why don't you? (*Offering the wicker fruit basket as* PHIL *heads off.*) Eat an orange, why don't you? Calm you down. (*Seeing that the basket is empty, he turns it over and out fall leaves, old grape stems.*) We need some fruit in this house. Where's the fruit? (*As* MICKEY *looks in the refrigerator,* EDDIE *has spread a line of coke on the coffee table.*) Where's the food? We need some food in this house. Eddie, where's all the food? (*Seeing* EDDIE *preparing to snort some cocaine.*) What are you doing?

EDDIE: What's it look like I'm doin'?

MICKEY: It looks like you are doin' a line of coke over there at eight forty-five in the morning.

EDDIE: Very good.
   (EDDIE *snorts coke, setting some out for* PHIL, *the two of them clearly in a conspiracy against* MICKEY; *almost like two bad little boys with a baby-sitter they don't care for.*)

MICKEY: What are you becoming, a coke fiend, Eddie?

EDDIE: How'm I gonna wake up? I gotta wake up!

MICKEY: Some people have coffee. (*With coffee on a spoon about to be dumped into the cup.*)

EDDIE: The caffeine is fucking poison, don't you know that?

MICKEY: Right. So what is this, Bolivian health food? Some people risk it with coffee to wake up in the morning, rather than this shit which can make you totally chemically insane. Don't you watch the six o'clock news?

EDDIE: I watch all the news.

MICKEY (*turning over the sugar tin, out falls a tattered, wrinkled package of pink Sno Balls, one and a half Sno Balls remaining, which he waves with a flourish*): Sno Balls! I found some fucking Sno Balls. All right, we can have some Sno Balls for breakfast. We can have some moldy Sno Balls along with our Bolivian Blow for breakfast. How long have I slept? Last time I saw you, you were a relatively standard everyday alcoholic Yahoo, Eddie. Now all I can find for breakfast is densely compressed chemicals and you're sniffin' around the living room like a wart hog.

EDDIE (*preparing to snort*): I had a rough night. Whata you want from me?

MICKEY: You should go to bed. (MICKEY *is cutting a Sno Ball, putting butter on it.*)

EDDIE: How'm I going to get to bed?

MICKEY: I don't know. Most people manage it. I don't know. Is this an outrageous suggestion, that he should get to bed? He's down here half the night, Phil, crashing around and talking to the TV like a goddamn maniac. Want half a dead Sno Ball, Phil? (*Gesturing an offer of a buttered Sno Ball on a plate to* PHIL, *who looks at* EDDIE, *and* MICKEY *shifts toward* EDDIE.) Eddie?

EDDIE (*clearly snubbing* MICKEY, EDDIE *turns to* PHIL, *who is spooning coke from the vial*): I gotta wake up. (*As* PHIL *puts the coke to one of* EDDIE's *nostrils.*) I got a lot of work today. (PHIL *puts coke to* EDDIE's *other nostril and*

EDDIE *snorts, then grabs* PHIL'S *face between his hands.*) The shit that went down here last night was conspiratorial. (EDDIE *leaps to his feet, putting on his glasses and grabbing the newspaper from the end table. Jolted with the coke, he is a whirlwind of information.*) First of all the eleven o'clock news has just devastated me with this shitload of horror in which it sounds like not only are we headed for nuclear devastation if not by the Russians then by some goddamn primitive bunch of Middle-Eastern motherfuckers— (*pacing behind the couch, he roots through the paper, while* PHIL *watches, and* MICKEY, *abandoned in the kitchen nook, eats the Sno Ball*) —and I don't mean that racially but just culturally, because they are so far back in the forest in some part of their goddamn mental sophistication, they are likely to drop the bomb just to see the light and hear the big noise. I mean, I am talking not innate ability, but sophistication here. They have got to get off the camels and wake up! (*Handing the newspaper to* PHIL, EDDIE *starts up the stairs.*) So on top of this, there's this accidental electrical fire in which an entire family is incinerated, the father trying to save everybody by hurling them out the window, but he's on the sixth floor, so they're like eggs on the sidewalk. So much for heroics. So then my wife calls! You wanna have some absurdity?

PHIL: I thought you was divorced.

EDDIE: I am.

PHIL (*tossing aside the newspaper, he moves toward the balcony to look up at* EDDIE, *who has paused near his door*): You said, "wife."

EDDIE: Why would I do that? I hate my ex-wife. I might have said "mother" instead of "ex-wife," but not "wife."

PHIL: Why would you do THAT?

EDDIE: Because I could have made a Freudian slip!

PHIL: You don't believe in that shit, do you?

EDDIE: Whata you know about it?

PHIL: Somethin'. I know somethin'. I was in prison.

EDDIE (*going into his room*): Mickey, what'd I say?

MICKEY: I wasn't listening.

PHIL (*yelling after* EDDIE): I mean, how would that shit work? You'd have WHAT?—all that stuff from your neighborhood like chasing you?

MICKEY: You mean like from your background.

PHIL: You believe in that Freudian shit, Mickey?

MICKEY: What Freudian shit?

PHIL: You know. All those books!

MICKEY: No.

PHIL: Me neither. (*Crossing to the kitchen to join* MICKEY.) I mean, how would that work? What? Ghosts?

MICKEY: It wouldn't.

PHIL: So assholes pay all this money, right. (PHIL *is laughing with* MICKEY *as* EDDIE, *having come out of his room, is pulling on a raggedy sweatshirt to wear with his raggedy,*

cut-off sweatpants. He moves to descend the stairs.) It's
unbelievable; and it don't work.

MICKEY: Eddie's done it.

PHIL: You done it, Eddie?

EDDIE *(picking up the newspaper, he sits down on the couch)*:
What?

PHIL: What we're talkin' about here. You were just talkin'
about it, too!

MICKEY: Freud.

EDDIE: Right. A pioneer. One of the real prestige guys of blow.
*(And opening the paper wide before his face, he disap-
pears behind it, closing the conversation, leaving* PHIL
and MICKEY *seated on either side of the counter, looking
at him.)*

MICKEY: So, Phil, your personal life's a shambles. *(*PHIL *turns
to look at* MICKEY.*)* How's your career?

PHIL: I'm up for some very interesting parts at the moment,
and on several of them—my agent says on this new cop
show for NBC, my agent says I'm a lock, that's how close
I am. I been back six times; the director and I have hit it
off. It's very exciting.

MICKEY: Who's the director?

PHIL: He's this terrific Thomas Leighton.

EDDIE *(quite exasperated, he violently shuts the newspaper)*:
This is the Thomas Leighton thing?! *(This is clearly a*

topic with a history between EDDIE *and* PHIL. EDDIE
heads toward the counter.) He's a scumbag. I tol' you,
Phil. He's a scumbag faggot who likes to jerk tough guys
like you around. He'll bring you back a hundred times,
you'll get nothing. (*On the upstage side of the counter,
he leans between them, separating them.*)

PHIL (*a little distressed that* EDDIE *is saying these things in
front of* MICKEY): My agent says he likes me, and it's
between me and this other guy who is taller, and that the
only problem is when they cast the lead, if he's a different type than me, then I'll have a very good shot.

EDDIE: The leads are always a different physical type than
you, Phil. This is America. This is TV.

PHIL: What are you tryin' to discourage me for?

EDDIE: I'm not trying to discourage you.

MICKEY (*rising*): This is Eddie's particular talent—to ef-
fortlessly discourage people. (*As* PHIL *rises and moves
down toward the armchair where his coat hangs.*)

EDDIE:
(MICKEY *is moving to climb the stairs.*)

If Phil wants to obliquely pick my brain about our area
of expertise here, Mickey, am I supposed to pretend that
you and I are not casting directors or I haven't noticed
the whys and wherefores of how the thing happens in
this town? That's what he's after. Right, Phil? (*Following
down to* PHIL, *who is putting on his jacket by the chair.*)

PHIL: I mean, Eddie, I trust that you are not deliberately
trying to discourage me, but in all honesty, I gotta tell

you, I'm feelin' very discouraged. (*Putting on his sunglasses, he is going to leave. On his way to the door, he pauses at the coffee table to pick in an ashtray for a leftover joint.*)

EDDIE: No, no. (*Moving upstage to head* PHIL *off before he can get to the door.*) Look, you have to exploit your marketable human qualities, that's all. You have certain qualities and you have to exploit them. I mean, basically we all know the M.O. out here is they take an interesting story, right? (*From off the stairway, he grabs a manuscript; using it as an example, he waves it at* PHIL.) They distort it, right? Cut whatever little truth there might be in it out on the basis of it's unappealing, but leave the surface so it looks familiar—cars, hats, trucks, trees. So, they got their scam, but to push it they have to flesh it out. So this is where you come in. (*He has* PHIL'*s attention now.*) Because then they need a lot of authentic-sounding and -looking people—high-quality people such as yourself, who need a buck.
(*Taking off the sunglasses,* PHIL *is ready to stay.*)

So like every other whore in this town, myself included, you have to learn to lend your little dab of whatever truth you can scrounge up in yourself to this total, this systematic sham—so that the fucking viewer will be exonerated from ever having to confront directly the fact that he is spending his life face to face with total shit. (*Pacing off from* PHIL *now,* EDDIE *is at the TV.*) So that's all I'm sayin'. "Check with me," is all I'm sayin'. Forget about this Leighton thing. (*He flops down on the couch, the script still in his hand.*)

PHIL (*moving up behind the couch*): Forget about it? I got nothin' else to do. What about the things you're currently working on? Anything for me?

MICKEY (*descending the steps, dressed for work, and carrying a handful of résumés and photographs*): Nothing.

PHIL: Who asked you?
(MICKEY *settles down at the end of the kitchen counter by the phone.*)

EDDIE: There's this thing down the road a month or so, it might be a good thing for you. (*He drops the script onto the couch.*)

PHIL: What is it?

EDDIE: It's a special or a pilot, they haven't decided. (*Picking a joint from the ashtray, he prepares to light up.*)

PHIL (*pacing behind the couch, peeking at the script* EDDIE *has tossed aside*): But there might be somethin' in it for me. Is that the script?

EDDIE: This is shit, though. (*He hands* PHIL *the script.*) I don't wanna hear about the quality, because this is total shit. That's just the way it is now, Phil, but it ain't always gonna be this way. We maneuver them, they maneuver us, but the day comes when we are positioned to make somethin' decent insteada this kinda delusionary crapola. (*Having lain back on the couch, he inhales the joint.*)

MICKEY (*dropping a pile of résumés into the waste can*): Don't get fucked up, Eddie. We got that meeting in less than two hours.

PHIL (*leafing through the script*): This is shit, huh?

EDDIE: Total.

PHIL: But there might be somethin' in it for me?

EDDIE: Yeah.
(PHIL *starts off.* EDDIE *sits up, fearful* PHIL's *feelings have been hurt again.*)

Where you goin'?

PHIL (*indicating the stairs*): I'm going to read it. And also, I'm beat. I'm really beat. It's been one exhausting thing I went through. I'm gonna pass out in your room, Eddie, okay?

EDDIE (*as* PHIL *is going up the stairs*): We'll do something later. (EDDIE *takes a huge toke on the joint as he lies back down.*)

MICKEY: Do you realize, Eddie, that you are now toking up at eight fifty-eight in the morning on top of the shit you already put up your nose. (*Taking the joint from* EDDIE's *mouth,* MICKEY *hands him a pile of résumés.*) You're going to show up at work looking like you got a radish for a nose. You're going to show up talking like a fish.

EDDIE: You don't have to worry about me, Mickey.

MICKEY (*sitting down in the armchair, he sorts the résumés*): What kind of tone is that?

EDDIE: What do you mean, what kind of tone is that? That's my tone. (*Relighting the joint, he nevertheless starts to look at the résumés.*)

MICKEY: So what does it mean?

EDDIE: My tone? What does my tone mean? I don't have to

interpret my fucking tone to you, Mickey. I don't know what it means. What do you think it means?

MICKEY: Just don't get clandestine on me, Eddie; that's all I'm saying.

EDDIE (*hurling the résumés onto the floor*): But there are not a lot of dynamite ladies around anywhere you look, Mickey, as we both know, and I am the one who met Darlene first. I am the one who brought her by, and it was obvious right from the get-go that Darlene was a dynamite lady, this was a very special lady.

MICKEY: We hit it off, Eddie, you know. I asked you.

EDDIE: Absolutely. Look, I'm not claiming any reprehensible behavior on anybody's part, but don't ask me not to have my feelings hurt, okay. I mean, we are all sophisticated people, and Darlene and I most certainly had no exclusive commitment of any kind whatsoever to each other, blah-blah-blah.

MICKEY: That's exactly what I'm saying. Rapateta.

EDDIE: There's no confusion here, Mickey, but have a little empathy for crissake.
(MICKEY *nods, for "empathy" is certainly something he can afford to give, and then he starts to pick up the scattered résumés.*)

I bring this very special lady to my house to meet my roommate, my best friend, and I haven't been seriously interested in a woman for a long time, I have this horror show of a marriage in my background, and everybody knows it, so blah-blah-blah, they have THIS ATTRACTION to each other.

(*Seeing now that* EDDIE *is after more than "empathy,"* MICKEY *shakes his head in mock dismay.*)

My roommate and my new girl—I'm just trying to tell the story here, Mickey; nobody's to blame. Certainly not you.
(*Putting the retrieved résumés on the coffee table,* MICKEY *sits back down on the armchair.*)

I mean, you came to me, you had experienced these vibes between yourself and Darlene—isn't that what you said? I mean, you correct me if I'm wrong—but would I mind, you wondered, if you and Darlene had dinner in order to, you know, determine the nature of these vibes, or would that bother me? (*Advancing on* MICKEY.) That's a fair—I mean, reasonable—representation of what you asked.

MICKEY (*heading for the kitchen,* EDDIE *following him*): I just—I mean, from my point of view, the point is—the main point is, I asked.

EDDIE: I know this.

MICKEY: That—in my opinion—is the paramount issue, the crucial issue. And I don't want it forgotten.

EDDIE: Nothing from yesterday is forgotten, Mickey. You don't have to worry about that.

MICKEY (*grabbing his coffee along with a plate with a part of a Sno Ball on it and his résumés and a script, he heads for the couch*): Why do we have to go through this? I just wanna have some breakfast. I mean, couldn't you have said, "no"? Couldn't you have categorically, definitively said "no" when I asked? But you said, "Everybody's free, Mickey." That's what you said.

EDDIE: Everybody is free.

MICKEY: So what's this then?

EDDIE: This? You mean this? This conversation?

MICKEY: Yeah. (*Having reached the couch, he sits, trying to work as* EDDIE *leans against the stairway near the landing.*)

EDDIE: This is JUST ME trying to maintain a, you know, viable relationship with reality. I'm just trying to make certain I haven't drifted off into some, you know, solitary paranoid fantasy system of my own, totally unfounded and idiosyncratic invention. I'm just trying to stay in reality, Mickey, that's all. Don't you want me to be in reality? I personally want us both to be in reality.

MICKEY: Absolutely. That's what I want. I mean, I want us both to be in reality. Absolutely.

EDDIE (*very reassuring as he moves to put out the joint, take up his pile of résumés and sit beside* MICKEY): So that's what's going on here, you know, blah-blah-blah. Don't take it personally.

MICKEY: Blah-blah-blah! Rapateta.
(*For a second, they sit there, working.*)

EDDIE: So I was just wondering. You came in this morning at something like six-oh-two, so your dinner must have been quite successful. These vibes must have been serious. I mean, sustaining, right?

MICKEY: Right. Yeah. You know.

EDDIE: Or does it mean—and I'm just trying to get the facts straight here, Mickey—does it mean you fucked her?

MICKEY (*slamming shut the script*): Darlene?

EDDIE: Right.

MICKEY: Darlene? Did I fuck Darlene? Last night? Eddie, hey, I asked you. I thought we were clear on this thing.

EDDIE: We're almost clear.

MICKEY (*with a take-charge manner, as if he has at last figured out what it is that* EDDIE *wants*): What I mean, Eddie is, THINGS HAPPEN, but if this bothers you, I mean, if this bothers you, I don't have to see her again. This is not worth our friendship, Eddie; you know that.

EDDIE: Wait a minute. You're not saying that you took my new girl, my very special dynamite girl out and fucked her on a whim, I mean, a fling, and it meant nothing!? You're not saying that?

MICKEY: No, no, no.

EDDIE: I mean, these vibes were serious, right? These vibes were the beginnings of something very serious, right? They were the first, faint, you know, things of a serious relationship, right?

MICKEY: Hey, whatever.

EDDIE: I mean, I don't want to interfere with any possibilities for happiness in your life, Mickey.

MICKEY: Believe me, this is not a possibility for happiness in my life.

EDDIE: Well, it was in mine. It was such a possibility in mine.

MICKEY: I think you just have it maybe all out of proportion here, Eddie.

EDDIE: Yeah? So do me a breakdown.

MICKEY: I just think maybe she's not as dynamite as you might think.
(EDDIE *nearly catapults across the room to the kitchen counter where the dope box sits.*)

EDDIE: Fuck you!

MICKEY: You always go a little crazy about women, Eddie.

EDDIE: You wanna let it alone, Mickey. (*He has taken a vial from the box and is dumping coke on his hand in order to snort it.*)

MICKEY: It's not a totally, you know, eccentric thing to happen to a guy, so don't get fucking defensive.

EDDIE: I mean, there's nothing here that necessitates any sort of underground smear campaign against Darlene. (*He snorts and heads toward the couch.*)

MICKEY: No, no, no. I just want you to think about the possibility that things have gotten a little distorted, that's all.

EDDIE: No.

MICKEY: You won't think about it?

EDDIE: I mean, bad-mouthing her just to get yourself off the hook—don't think you can do that.

MICKEY: Never.

EDDIE: It's not that I DON'T understand—it's that I DO understand. It's just that I'm not so fucking sophisticated as to be totally beyond this entire thing, you see what I'm saying, Mickey. Blah-blah-blah—my heart is broken—blah-blah-blah. (*At the couch, he snorts again and flops down on the couch, grabbing a pillow, which he hugs.*)

MICKEY: Blah-blah-blah. Absolutely. So you want me to toast you what's left of the Sno Ball here? We can put some raisins on it—be sort of Danish. Somebody's got to go shopping.

EDDIE (*lying forlornly on the couch, hugging his pillow*): You think we couldn't handle a dog around here?

MICKEY: I wouldn't want to be a fucking dog around here. Dogs need stability.

EDDIE: I like dogs.

MICKEY: You could borrow Artie's dog.

EDDIE: I hate Artie's dog. It looks like a rat; it doesn't look like a dog. I like big dogs.

MICKEY (*crossing with the Sno Ball on a plate, he picks and eats a piece before handing the plate with the remainder to* EDDIE): So did you get any sleep at all?

EDDIE: Fucking Agnes had to call. Why does she have to call?

MICKEY: Why do you talk to her is the real question.

EDDIE: I have to talk to her. We have a kid.

MICKEY: I mean, it's ridiculous.
(*He heads for the kitchen, and as he does, the door opens behind him and* ARTIE *comes in,* DONNA *with him.* EDDIE, *turned away on the couch, doesn't see them, nor does* MICKEY, *his back turned as he heads to the refrigerator.*)

You might as well put your balls in her teeth as pick up the phone.

EDDIE: Because she thinks she's smarter than me, I pick up the phone.

MICKEY: And then you go crazy for days!
(ARTIE, *looking back and forth between* EDDIE *and* MICKEY, *goes to the counter, where he nibbles a hunk of Sno Ball while* DONNA *hovers by the door.*)

EDDIE: What do you want me to do, abandon my kid in her hands with no other hope? Forget about it!
(ARTIE *is about ten years older than* EDDIE *and* MICKEY. *He is slick in appearance, dressed very California; a mix of toughness and arrogance, a cunning desperation; he carries a shoulder satchel.* DONNA *is blonde, about sixteen. She wears a knapsack. Under her arm she has a record album, which she will carry everywhere. She wears tattered shorts, a T-shirt, a tattered athletic jacket and beat-up high-top sneakers. Turning from the refrigerator,* MICKEY *sees* ARTIE, *and addresses him as if he's been standing there for years.*)

MICKEY: Artie, so what's the haps, here?

ARTIE: You guys in the middle of something, or what? (*As* DONNA *comes running forward to join* ARTIE.)

MICKEY: You didn't tell us you got married.

ARTIE: Her? I found her on the elevator.

DONNA: Where's the bathroom?

EDDIE (*still lying on his belly on the couch, almost like he is talking in his sleep*): What kind of accent is that? What kind of accent you got?

DONNA: I'm from the Midwest, so that's it.

ARTIE (*to* MICKEY): You want her?

MICKEY: Whata you mean?

ARTIE: It's too crowded, see?

DONNA: Artie, they got a bathroom?

ARTIE: Sure they got a bathroom.

EDDIE (*from the couch*): What's she want with our bathroom, Artie? Is this a goddamn coke fiend you brought with you here?

DONNA: I gotta go.

EDDIE: Where?

DONNA: I gotta go to the bathroom.

ARTIE: This is Eddie.

DONNA: Hi, you got a bathroom?

EDDIE: It's upstairs.

DONNA: Great.

MICKEY (*as* DONNA *hurries up the stairs*): I'm Mickey. It's the first door.

DONNA: Great, Mickey. I'm Donna. (*She goes into the bathroom, shutting the door.*)

MICKEY: Cute, Artie, very cute.

ARTIE (*to* MICKEY): You want her?

EDDIE: You keep sayin' that, Artie.

ARTIE (*as if irritated at her*): She was on the goddamn elevator. In the hotel. I'm going out for coffee in the morning, I take the elevator, there she is.

MICKEY (*moving to get* ARTIE *some coffee*): You want coffee? We got coffee, Sno Balls, coke and raisins.

ARTIE (*glancing at his watch, he settles into the swivel chair in front of the counter*): It's too early for breakfast, but I'll have some coffee. This was yesterday. So I come back from coffee, she's in the elevator. It's an hour. So that's a coincidence. Then I'm going out for dinner. Right? This is seven-eight hours later. She's in the elevator.

MICKEY: She's livin' in the elevator.

ARTIE: Yeah, so after dinner, there she is. So I ask her: Is she livin' in the elevator? She says her boyfriend tried to kill her, so she's stayin' off the street.

MICKEY (*handing* ARTIE *the coffee*): Why'd he want to kill her?

ARTIE: She says he was moody. So I took her in. But I figured, I don't need her, you know, like you guys need her. You guys are a bunch of desperate guys. You're very desperate guys, right? You can use her. So I figured on my way to the studio, I'd drop her by, you can keep her. Like a CARE package, you know. So you can't say I never gave you nothing.

EDDIE (*from the couch*): You're giving her to us?

ARTIE: Yeah.

EDDIE: What are we going to do with her?

ARTIE: What do you want to do with her?

EDDIE: Where's she from?

MICKEY (*as if* EDDIE *is an imbecile*): What has that got to do with anything?

EDDIE: I wanna know.

MICKEY: Somewhere in the Middle West. I heard her.

EDDIE: That could be anywhere.

MICKEY: So what?

EDDIE: I'm just trying to figure out what we're going to do with her. You wanna pay attention.

ARTIE (*intervening on* MICKEY's *behalf, he crosses toward* EDDIE): What do you want, Eddie, an instruction manual? This is a perfectly viable piece of ass I have brought you, and you're acting totally like WHAT? What's going on here? Are we in sync or not?

EDDIE: Like she'll be a pet, is that what you're saying, Artie?

ARTIE: Right.

MICKEY: Right.

ARTIE: You can keep her around. (*Heading back toward the counter where he left his coffee.*)

EDDIE (*following* ARTIE): She'll be like this pet we can keep and fuck her if we want to?

ARTIE: Sure. Just to stay in practice. In case you run into a woman.

EDDIE: I guess he hasn't heard about Darlene. I guess you haven't heard about Darlene, Artie.

ARTIE: No. Is this important?

EDDIE (*moving around the back of the counter, he insinuates himself between* MICKEY *and* ARTIE): Mickey has gotten involved with this truly dynamite bitch in a very serious relationship.

MICKEY: Bullshit. (*Bolting to the couch where he has left his work.*)

ARTIE: Is this true, Mickey? (*As* EDDIE, *following* MICKEY, *is halted by* ARTIE.) Is this the same Darlene, Eddie? You had a Darlene.

EDDIE: What I'm inferring here, Artie, is that Mickey is unlikely to be interested in this bimbo you have brought by for fear of, you know, contaminating his feelings and catching some vile disease in addition.

ARTIE: So when did this happen, Mickey? (ARTIE *moves to join* MICKEY, *while* EDDIE *loiters near the stairway land-*

ing.) You guys switched, or what? I miss everything. So you're in a serious relationship, Mickey. That's terrific.

MICKEY: Except I ain't serious about anything, Artie, you know that. (*As* DONNA, *clumping down the stairs, comes face to face with* EDDIE.)

EDDIE: You wanna live with us for a while, Donna?

DONNA: Hmmmmmmmmmmmmm?

ARTIE: Okay, I gotta go. (*Crossing to the counter where he left his briefcase.*) All she has to do for me is go down to the hotel twice a day and walk my dog.

MICKEY: Right.

EDDIE (*as* DONNA *bolts past* EDDIE *to get close to* ARTIE, *clearly hoping to leave with him*): What if she runs away?

ARTIE: What do you want from me, Eddie, a guarantee? (*Draping an arm over her shoulder,* ARTIE *hugs her, snuggling, possessing her.*) I can't guarantee her. She worked last time I used her. You want a guarantee, talk to the manufacturer. I'm not the manufacturer.

EDDIE (*settling down on the swivel chair in his raggedy gym clothes, he picks up the phone*): You're the retailer.

ARTIE: Frankly, from the look of you, what I am is a goddamn charity organization having some compassion on some pathetic fuck who is you, that's what I am. I'm having some generosity toward the heartbreaking desperation I encounter every time I come by and have to look at you. (ARTIE *shoves* DONNA *to* EDDIE, *setting her on his lap.*)

You don't mind if I have a little mercy. (*And turns to leave.*)

EDDIE: So where you goin' so early this morning? You goin' to the studio?

ARTIE: I said that. (*Rooting through his papers and briefcase, this is all swagger, toughness and mockery between* EDDIE *and* ARTIE.)

EDDIE: You didn't say what for.

ARTIE: You didn't ask what for. I got a meeting.

EDDIE (*with* DONNA *on his lap, he starts to look through the contents of her knapsack*): You know what happens to you doesn't happen to normal people.

ARTIE: I did good deeds in an earlier lifetime. How do I know?

EDDIE: Yeah, but being a highly developed bullshit artist does not normally translate into this kind of situation.

ARTIE: He's a blocked writer, and my stories about my life unblock him. You know, it was his idea and secretly I always dreamed of it. (*Holding up a manuscript.*)

EDDIE: You got a deal, right?

ARTIE: Things look VERY good. (*Packed now, he is heading for the door.*) They look VERY good. You know, who can tell in this town?

EDDIE: Did they write the check? If they wrote the check, you got a deal.

ARTIE: So they didn't. (*In the alcove, he turns back.*)

EDDIE: Then you don't.

ARTIE: YET. They didn't YET.

EDDIE (*enjoying himself,* EDDIE *is almost dancing forward*): Then you don't YET. If they didn't YET, you don't YET.

ARTIE: But we're close. We're very close.

EDDIE: The game in this town is not horseshoes, Artie.

ARTIE (*rushing back to* EDDIE, *who is just upstage of the armchair*): How come you're being such a prick to me?

EDDIE: Envy!

ARTIE: I didn't think you knew.

EDDIE: Of course I know. What do you think, I don't know what I'm feeling?

ARTIE: It happens.

EDDIE: Everything happens. (*Moving to the armchair where he sits, picking up a* Variety.) But what I'm after here, I mean ultimately, is for your own good, for your clarity. You lose your clarity in this town next thing you know you're waking up in the middle of the night on the beach with dogs pissing on you, you think you're on vacation. You panic in this town, Artie, they can smell it in your sweat.

ARTIE: Who's gonna panic? I been learning these incredible, fantastic relaxation techniques.

EDDIE: Who's the producer you're most often in the room with?

ARTIE: Simon! He's got a distribution deal now with Universal.

MICKEY: What relaxation techniques?

ARTIE (*sitting down beside* MICKEY *to demonstrate*): They are these ones that are fantastic, Mickey, in as much as you can do them under the table, you're in some goddamn meeting, you just tense your feet and hands, press 'em flat on the table and breathe and let the air—

EDDIE: HERB Simon?!! (*Hurling down the magazine, he pivots the chair to face* ARTIE.) HERB Simon? Is this who we're talking about?

ARTIE: What about him?

EDDIE (*leaping to his feet, he rushes at* ARTIE): He's a known snake! I got the right guy—Herb Simon.

ARTIE: Yeah. Universal.

EDDIE: HE'S AN ANACONDA. HE'S A KNOWN ANACONDA.

ARTIE (*shrugging*): I heard that.

EDDIE: These fucking snakes are sharks out here!

MICKEY: He's right, Artie.

ARTIE (*starting to try to do his relaxation technique*): We have hit it off. He likes me.

MICKEY: Good.

EDDIE: If it's true, it's good.

ARTIE: Fuck you! The guy is at this juncture where he's sick of himself; he's looking for some kind of turnaround into decency.

EDDIE: You base this opinion on what, Artie, your desperate desire to succeed?

ARTIE: Something happened and I saw it, goddammit.

MICKEY: So what happened?

ARTIE (*to* MICKEY): It was the other day after lunch.

EDDIE: Who paid?

ARTIE (*snapping at* EDDIE, *snarling, his relaxation technique having turned him into a knot of tension*): He did! He paid! (*He collapses, giving up on the technique.*) So we're crossing the street. You know, he gets this terrible pain in his stomach. I mean, his stomach made a noise and he doubles over like this. It's a noise like a gorilla could have made it. And he's over like this and he's paralyzed. We're all paralyzed in the middle of the street. So we get across the street. I'm asking him, is he okay. Maybe the food was bad. "No," he says. "Maybe," I says. "No. It's all the lies I tell," he says. He looks me in the eye and says, "It's this town and all the lies it makes me tell." See? He tol' me that.

EDDIE: So?

ARTIE: So, he was straight with me, you cynical prick.

EDDIE: So what's the point? This fucking snake tells you he lies a lot, so you figure you can trust him?! That's not clear, Artie. Wake up! This guy is legendary among snakes. He is permanently enshrined in the reptilian hall of Hollywood fucking fame, this guy. You don't wake up, they are going to eat you alive. As an appetizer! You won't even be the main course. They're just going to whet their appetites on what is to you your entire motherfucking existence.

ARTIE: You're making me nervous.

EDDIE: I'm trying to make you nervous. Don't you know a ploy when you see one?

ARTIE: I considered whether it was a ploy, and I come down on the side of I would trust him a little.

EDDIE: Why trust him at all?

ARTIE: I gotta work with him. (*Suddenly an alarm on* ARTIE'S *watch goes off and he leaps up, gathering his things.*)

EDDIE: I'm not sayin' "Don't work with him," I'm sayin' "Don't trust him." Get some money, get some bucks.

ARTIE: For crissake, I'm gonna be late with this bullshit you put me through. What do you do this to me for? He's gonna be pissed at me, goddammit! (*He rushes out the door.*)

DONNA: Bye, Artie. (*Having sat all this while on the kitchen stool where* EDDIE *was seated when* ARTIE *gave* DONNA *to him,* DONNA *now runs a few steps after* ARTIE, *but she falters.* ARTIE *is clearly not interested and* EDDIE *is there.*)

EDDIE: You think I was too hard on him?

MICKEY: No.

EDDIE: You gotta be hard on him, right?—he's a hardhead himself.

MICKEY: So how is Goldilocks, here? (*Having lit a joint, stretches on the couch to offer the joint to* DONNA.) You had any breakfast?

EDDIE (*watching* MICKEY *closely*): You want a beer?

DONNA (*having stepped toward* MICKEY, *she now steps toward* EDDIE, *who is headed for the refrigerator*): Sure.

EDDIE: Where'd you say you were from?

MICKEY (*as if very interested*): She said Midwest. I remember. Isn't that what you said?

DONNA: Yeah. (*Stepping back toward* MICKEY.)

MICKEY: See.

EDDIE: So you came out here to get into the movies? (*He leans against the kitchen counter, holding her beer; she steps back toward him.*)

DONNA: We were hitchhiking.

MICKEY: Where to?
(*Now she steps toward* MICKEY.)

DONNA: The Grand Canyon.

EDDIE: It's not in L.A.

DONNA: I just kept going.

Mickey: So you were in Artie's elevator?
    (*At last she gets the joint.*)

Donna: It wasn't his. Can I turn on the TV?

Eddie (*imitating her accent*): Sure.
    (Donna *scurries to the TV, which she turns on with the
    remote, and then she sits on the couch in front of the TV,
    which puts her beside* Mickey.)

    So if Artie hadn't invited you off the elevator, would you
    still be on it?!

Donna: I saw some interesting things I was on it! (*She
    smokes the joint greedily.*)

Mickey (*yelling over the loud volume of the TV*): Like what?!

Donna (*yelling*): Different people!

Eddie (*yelling from across the room*): This was interesting!
    (*As* Mickey *starts removing* Donna's *shoes.*)

Donna (*yelling*): You could hear their conversation! Some
    were about their rooms and the hotel carpeting, or the
    pictures in the hall! There was sometimes desperation
    you couldn't get a handle on it! They talked about their
    clothes!
    (Mickey, *with the remote, turns off the volume of the TV
    and moves to embrace her, kissing her neck as* Eddie
    moves in behind the couch.)

Mickey: So you evidently would have starved to death mes-
    merized by the spellbinding panorama on this elevator,
    it wasn't for Artie.

DONNA: I'da got off to eat. That's crazy. Did he say what time I should walk his dog? (*As she is almost settling into* MICKEY*'s embrace,* EDDIE *reaches to take the record album, which she has not let out of her grasp for a single second.*)

EDDIE: What's this?

DONNA: It's just my favorite record for very particular reasons. (*Lunging, she tries to retrieve the album, but* EDDIE *eludes her.* MICKEY *grabs the loose end of her jacket to stop her and pull her gently back.*)

EDDIE: Willie Nelson sings "Stardust," "Unchained Melody," "All of Me"?

DONNA: Nobody ever agrees with me, people just scream at me. (*On her knees on the couch, she talks to* MICKEY.)

MICKEY: What?

DONNA (MICKEY *pulls her gently back, his arm around her, and as she talks and he takes off her jacket,* EDDIE *eases onto the couch*): My friends, when I argue with them, they just scream at me, but it's these really terrific old songs sung by this new guy, right, Willie Nelson, only he's an old guy, and they're all like these big-city songs like Chicago or New York, right, Sinatra kind of songs, only Willie, who they are sung by, is this cowboy, so it's like this cowboy on the plains singing to his cows, and the mountains are there but it's still the deep, dark city streets, so it's like the mountains and the big sky are this nightclub in the night and this old cowboy, this old, old cowboy under a streetlight in the middle of the mountains is singing something old and modern, and it's everything, see. (*Looking at* EDDIE:) You wanna hear it?

EDDIE: No.

MICKEY: Sure. (*As* EDDIE's *bedroom door opens and* PHIL *steps out, his hair tousled, his shirt off.*)

PHIL: Anybody got any Valium around here, Eddie?

EDDIE (*he leaps to his feet, indicating* DONNA): Look at this. Artie brought her by.

PHIL: Where's Artie?

MICKEY: He's gone.

PHIL: Artie was here?

EDDIE: Yeah.

PHIL: Who's this?

EDDIE: He brought her by for us. Like a CARE package.

PHIL: Yeah? Whata you mean?

EDDIE (*reaching,* EDDIE *takes* MICKEY's *arm and lifts it off* DONNA): Not for Mickey, though.

MICKEY: Get off my back, you— (*Certain it's a joke, he reaches again, but* EDDIE *knocks* MICKEY's *hand once more aside.*)

EDDIE: This is for Phil and me because we don't have any serious relationships. This is a CARE package. Didn't you hear him? This is a CARE package for people without serious relationships. (*Having lifted* DONNA *into his own arms.*)

MICKEY: You prick.

DONNA: What're you guys talking about?

EDDIE: Fucking you.

DONNA: Oh.

EDDIE: Phil and me, but not Mickey because he has a serious relationship. He has to preserve it.

DONNA: You gotta work at it, Mickey.

PHIL: You're sayin' seriously this is includin' me?

EDDIE: So we'll go upstairs, okay, Donna?

DONNA: Okay. (*She grabs her record as they head for the stairs.*)

PHIL: He can't, but I can?

EDDIE: Yeah.

MICKEY: You sonofabitch. (MICKEY *is about to follow up the stairs.*)

EDDIE (*whirling on the the stairs to face* MICKEY): Don't you even think about it. Right, Phil?

MICKEY: I'll— (*Looking up,* MICKEY *meets* PHIL's *eyes.*) You jerk-off, Eddie! You jerk-off! I'll get her sometime you're not around.

EDDIE: I can only do so much for you, Mickey. That'll be on your conscience.

MICKEY: Give me a break. (*Rushing around, gathering up his script, his résumés and zipper folder in which he will carry them, as* EDDIE *and* DONNA *bound up the stairs.*)

EDDIE: This is for your own good.

PHIL: I got here just in time.

EDDIE (*looking down on* MICKEY): You'll thank me later! (*And whirling,* EDDIE *follows* DONNA *into his room.*)

MICKEY (*grabbing his jacket from where it hangs on a hook outside the closet door near the front door, he rushes out*): You're nuts, Eddie; you're fucking nuts!

PHIL: So this is the bachelor life!
(PHIL *goes into the bedroom, slamming the door, as the downstairs door slams, and the music starts: Willie Nelson singing "All of Me."*)

BLACKOUT

(*The music continues.*)

SCENE 2

Time: Evening of the same day.

Place: The same.

The music, Willie Nelson singing "All of Me," continues. The door opens and EDDIE *enters, carrying a paper and walking toward the kitchen. Almost simultaneously the bathroom door above him has opened and* DARLENE, *beautiful and fashionable, has come out, brushing her hair. She sees him and watches as he walks to the refrigerator. The music goes out.*

DARLENE: Hi.

EDDIE (*he whirls, startled to see her*): Hi, Darlene. (*He looks around.*) Mickey around?

DARLENE (*starting down the stairs*): I'm supposed to meet him. (*She pauses on the landing to look at him.*) Is it okay?

EDDIE: Sure. How you doing? You look good.

DARLENE: It's a facade.

51

EDDIE: What isn't? That's what I meant, you know. (*She comes down the stairs toward the armchair near which her purse sits on the floor. EDDIE opens the refrigerator and pulls out a beer.*) I wasn't saying anything more. It's a terrifically successful facade. (*He moves toward where she now sits in the armchair.*) So, how's life in the world of fashion photography, Darlene?

DARLENE: Can I have a beer, too?

EDDIE: Sure. (*He starts for the refrigerator.*)

DARLENE: I just feel . . .
(*The word "feel" spins him to look at her.*)

Wow . . . you know?

EDDIE: What?

DARLENE: Weird, weird, weird.

EDDIE: I mean, you're not giving this whole situation a second thought, are you?

DARLENE: I certainly am. I . . .

EDDIE: No, no, no. (*Crossing toward her.*)

DARLENE: What situation? What do you mean? Do you—

EDDIE: Us. Mickey, you, me. Us.

DARLENE: Of course I am. That's what I thought you meant.

EDDIE (*crossing behind her to sit on the arm of the couch*): Don't be crazy.

DARLENE: Well, I have my mad side, you know. I have my feelings.

EDDIE: I don't mean "mad" by "crazy." I mean, "mad" has a kind of grandeur about it. I mean more like "silly." (*Rising, he crosses to the phone, the Rolodex.*) Is that what I mean?

DARLENE: Well, if you don't know, maybe you should stop talking till you figure it out and not go around just spewing out all this incomprehensible whatever it is you're saying and, you know, hurting a person's feelings. That might have some value.

EDDIE: I opted for spontaneity, you know.

DARLENE: Well, sure. I'm just saying, "strike a balance."

EDDIE: I mean, we've all had our feelings hurt, Darlene. I hope you're conscious of the universal here.

DARLENE: What are you getting at?

EDDIE: I'm not exactly certain.

DARLENE: Well . . . are you exactly uncertain?

EDDIE: Possibly.

DARLENE: Where's Mickey? (*Leaping up, she crosses to the front door to look for* MICKEY.)

EDDIE: Is he late? Gee, he's usually so dependable.

DARLENE: This is a perfect example of what could drive a person right off the wall about you. I mean, you are totally off the wall sometimes.

EDDIE: In what way? Everybody has their flaws, Darlene.

DARLENE: This total way you exaggerate this enchantment you have with uncertainty—the way you just prolong it and expect us all to think we ought to try and live in it and it's meaningful. It's shit. (*Grabbing up her purse as he moves toward her and the armchair, she flees to the couch, where she sits, looking at her phone book.*)

EDDIE: This bothers you.

DARLENE: It bothers everyone.

EDDIE: No, it bothers you. (*Sitting down on the armchair.*) And don't think this is a surprise. I am well aware of how what might to another person appear as honesty, but to you, it's—

DARLENE: Some other person such as who?

EDDIE: You want a list?

DARLENE: I want an answer. And a beer.

EDDIE: The beer is in the refrigerator.
(*She storms past* EDDIE *to the refrigerator.*)

And the answer, if you want it from me, is coming along the lines I am speaking it, which is the only way it can come, since it's my answer, and if it is to come at all, it—

DARLENE (*she slams the refrigerator shut*): I don't have time. I mean, your thoughts are a goddamn caravan trekking the desert, and then they finally arrive and they are these senseless beasts of burden. Okay? (*Settling down on a stool outside the kitchen counter by the phone.*) So just forget about it.

EDDIE: You asked me a question.

DARLENE: I also asked you to forget about it. I made a mistake.

EDDIE (*moving toward her, his beer can raised for emphasis*):
But you don't deny you asked it.

DARLENE: Eddie, you look like a man with a hammer in his hand.

EDDIE: So what? And I don't. Or are you a liar on top of everything else? You asked me a question!

DARLENE: All right!

EDDIE: Some sensitivity is the quality a person might have. That's the quality a person might— (*Turning, he starts off toward the couch.*)

DARLENE: Liar on top of WHAT ELSE?

EDDIE: Whata you mean?

DARLENE: You said, "liar on top of everything else."

EDDIE: I did? (*Crossing back to her.*)

DARLENE: Just a second ago.

EDDIE: What was I talking about?

DARLENE: ME.

EDDIE: I did? No. What'd I say?

DARLENE: "LIAR ON TOP OF EVERYTHING ELSE!"
(*The front door opens, and* MICKEY, *carrying a bag of groceries, comes in. He has a six-pack of beer in one hand.*)

MICKEY: Hi.

DARLENE: Hi.

MICKEY: How you doing?

EDDIE: Great. You?

MICKEY (*moving to them, setting the bag on the counter*): Terrific. Anybody need a beer?

EDDIE: No.

DARLENE: Sure. (*Moving around* EDDIE, *she takes a beer from the offered six-pack and gives* MICKEY *a hug.* EDDIE *slips off to sit on the stool farthest to stage left.*)

MICKEY (*embracing* DARLENE): You know what I'm going to do? I'm going to venture a thought that I might regret down the road. And anticipating that regret makes me, you know, hesitate. (*Having pulled back from her, he sets her down on the stool, which puts her and* EDDIE *on the two stools on the downstage side of the counter.* MICKEY *crosses to* EDDIE.) In the second of hesitation, I get a good look at the real feeling that it is, this regret—a kind of inner blackmail that shows me even further down the road where I would end up having to live with myself as a smaller person, a man less generous to his friends than I would care to be. (*Crossing to* EDDIE.) So, you know, we'll have to put this through a multiprocessing here, but I was outside, I mean, for a while; and what I heard in here was—I mean, it really was passion. (*He*

settles back against the counter between them now.)
Sure, it was a squabble, and anybody could have heard
that, but what I heard was more. We all know—
everybody knows I'm basically on a goof right now. I'm
going back to my wife and kids sooner or later—I don't
hide that fact from anybody. And what I really think is
that fact was crucial to the development of this whole
thing because it made me WHAT? Safe. A viable diver-
sion from what might have actually been a genuine,
meaningful, and to that same extent and maybe even
more so—threatening—connection between you two.
I'm not going to pretend I wasn't up for it, too. But I was
never anything but above board. You know—a couple
jokes, nice dinner, that's my style. Good wine, we gotta
spend the night—and I don't mean to be crass—because
the point is maybe we have been made fools of here by
our own sophistication, and what am I protecting by not
saying something about it, my vanity? Ego? Who needs
it? (*Suddenly dashing up the stairs to his room, still
speaking, he pulls a small suitcase from his room.*) So,
I'm out in the yard and I'm thinking, "Here is this terrific guy, this dynamite lady, and they are obviously,
definitely hooked up on some powerful, idiosyncratic
channel, so what am I doing in the middle?" (*Back down
the stairs, he looks at* EDDIE.) Am I totally off base here,
Eddie, or what?

EDDIE: You're—I mean, obviously you're not TOTALLY. You
know that.

MICKEY: That's exactly what I'm saying.

EDDIE: I mean, from my end of it.

MICKEY (*moving behind the counter, he positions himself
between them*): For my own well-being, I don't want to
serve as the instrument of some neurotic, triangular

bullshit being created here between you two. That's the
main issue for me. I mean, from my point of view.

EDDIE: Right.

DARLENE (*leaning forward, trying to insert herself into their
attention*): I mean, I certainly haven't felt right—I
mean, good about it, that's—

MICKEY: Everything went so fast.

DARLENE: Everything just happened.

MICKEY: You met him, you met me.

DARLENE: I met Eddie, and then Eddie, you know, introduces
me to you.

EDDIE: It's too fast.

DARLENE: It was fast.

MICKEY: Just— What is this, the electronic age? Sure. But
we're people, not computers; the whole program cannot
be just reprogrammed without some resolution of the
initial, you know, thing that started everything. (*Having
hastened to the grocery bag, he is taking out a bottle of
wine and sticking it under his coat, all without either of
them seeing.*) So I'm going to—I don't know what—but
go. Somewhere. Out. And you two can just see where it
takes you. Go with the flow. (*Coming forward, he looks
at them.*) I mean, you guys should see yourselves.

DARLENE: I'm just—I mean, I don't— Weird, weird, weird.

MICKEY (*patting* DARLENE'S *hand*): In all honesty, Darlene,
you told me this is what you wanted in more ways than I

cared to pay attention to. (*Backing for the door, he looks at* EDDIE.) And you, you prick, you were obviously madly in love. (*To* DARLENE:) Go easy on him. I'll catch you later.

EDDIE: Down the road.

DARLENE: Bye.

MICKEY (*at the door, he slips on his sunglasses*): Just remember, Darlene, you made the wrong choice. (MICKEY *goes.*)

EDDIE: Where the hell did he come up with the . . . I mean, clarity to do that?

DARLENE: That wasn't clarity.

EDDIE: No, no, I mean, it wasn't clarity. But he had to HAVE clarity.

DARLENE: I don't know what it was. Generosity?

EDDIE: Whatever it was, you don't see it very often. I don't expect that from Mickey, I mean, that kind of thing.

DARLENE (*she bolts away, quite edgy and heading for the couch, where she will gather her things*): Who expects that from anybody? We're all so all over the place.

EDDIE: Self-absorbed.

DARLENE (*she's in quite an exasperated state*): And distracted. I'm distracted by everything. I mean, I'm almost always distracted by everything. I mean, I'm almost always distracted, aren't you?

EDDIE: Absolutely.

DARLENE (*angry at everything that has been distracting her*):
Everything is always distracting me from everything
else.

EDDIE (*following after her, he is angry at himself for being
such a distraction to himself*): Everything is very distracting, but what I've really noticed is that mainly, the
thing I'm most distracted by is myself. I mean, I'm my
own major distraction, trying to get it together, to get
my head together, my act together.

DARLENE: Our little minds just buzzzzzzzz! What do they
think they're doing? (*As she grabs up her purse and
seems about to leave, he grabs her arm. They are standing in front of the couch.*)

EDDIE: However Mickey managed to get through it, though. I
know one thing—I'm glad he did.

DARLENE (*sarcastically*): Are you really?

EDDIE: I really missed you. It was amazing.
(*She flops down on the couch.*)

That was probably it—he got his clue from the fact that I
never shut up about you. I think I was driving him crazy.
How do you feel?

DARLENE: Great. (*And he joins her.*) I think I was, you know,
into some form of obsession about you, too, some form
of mental loop. (*Kissing him, she suddenly pulls back.*) I
feel scared is what I feel. Good, too. I feel good, but
mainly scared. (*She bolts from the couch, around the
back, heading for the kitchen.*)

EDDIE: I'm scared. (*He moves the other way to head her off.*)

DARLENE: I mean, a year ago, I was a basket case. (*As he grabs her, stops her.*) If we had met a year ago, I wouldn't have had a prayer.

EDDIE: Me, too. (*He hugs her desperately.*) A year ago, I was nuts. And I still have all kinds of things to think through. (*He starts taking off her jacket.*) Stuff coming up, I have to think it through.

DARLENE: Me, too.

EDDIE (*backing her up, he sits her down on the arm of the couch to make his point as she is unbuttoning his shirt*): And by thinking, I don't mean just some ethereal mental thing either, but being with people is part of it, being with you is part of the thinking, that's how I'm doing the thinking, but I just have to go slow, there's a lot of scar tissue.

DARLENE: There's no rush, Eddie.

EDDIE (*taking off his jacket*): I don't want to rush.

DARLENE: I don't want to rush.

EDDIE (*as he moves forward, pressing her backward; together they go over onto the couch*): I can't rush. I'll panic. If I rush, I'll panic.

DARLENE: We'll just have to keep our hearts open, as best we can.

EDDIE: No pressure.

DARLENE: And no guilt, okay?

EDDIE: No guilt.

(*They kiss, and kissing roll over onto the floor,* DARLENE *ending up on top.*)

DARLENE (*pulling free and back*): We don't want any guilt. I mean, I'm going to be out of town a lot. We both have our lives.

EDDIE (*sitting up; both are now getting their clothes off*): We just have to keep our options open.

DARLENE: And our hearts, okay?

EDDIE: I mean, the right attitude . . .

DARLENE: Exactly. If we have the right attitude . . . (*Pulling off her camisole, she is in a bra.*)

EDDIE (*tearing at his shirt and shoes*): Attitude is so important. And by attitude I don't mean just attitude either, but I mean real emotional space.

DARLENE: We both need space.

EDDIE: And time. We have to have time. (*His shirt attached to him only by one buttoned sleeve, he kisses her.*)

DARLENE: Right. (*He is leaning her back onto the floor.*) So we can just take the time to allow the emotional space for things to grow and work themselves out.

EDDIE: So you wanna fuck?
(*She nods "yes." He kisses her. As music starts and lights BLACK OUT. The music is Willie Nelson singing "Someone to Watch Over Me."*)

SCENE 3

Time: Late afternoon of the next day.

Place: The same.

The music, Willie Nelson singing "Someone to Watch Over Me," continues. DONNA comes out of MICKEY's room, moving to the music; she descends the stairs, dancing over to the TV, which she turns on, the volume loud. Dancing, she flops down onto the couch. The door opens and PHIL comes in looking disheveled. He carries two six-packs of beer and grocery bags containing meat and bread for sandwiches and two huge bags of popcorn. Seeing her, he groans and starts talking immediately, almost like a man talking to himself.

PHIL: So this broad is always here, you know what I mean? What is she, a chair? What are you, a goddamn chair? You sit around here and you would let anybody do anything to you, wouldn't you? Whatsamatter with you? Don't you have any self-respect? You're all alike. She is!

DONNA: Who you talkin' to?

PHIL (yelling up the stairs toward EDDIE's room as he crosses *back toward the door to hang up his coat on the hook on the support beam*): She's got the goddamn TV on and the record player on! Who you workin' for, the electric company?

DONNA: Who you talkin' to, Phil?

PHIL: Don't call me Phil, okay. Just don't. I'm talkin' to you. Who asked you anyway?

DONNA: You ain't talkin' to me, I could tell by your tone. Who you talkin' to?

PHIL: You're very observant. You're very smart. Who was I talkin' to?

DONNA: I don't know. I'm the only one here.

PHIL: I was talkin' to Eddie.

DONNA: Eddie ain't here.

PHIL: He's up in his room.

DONNA: He ain't.

PHIL (*running partway up the stairs*): EDDIE! EDDIE! Where the hell are you? (*He hastens on to check into* EDDIE'S *room.*) I was just talkin' to him.

DONNA: That's what I been trying to explain to you.

PHIL (*moving from* EDDIE'S *room to look into the bathroom and* MICKEY'S *room*): Get off my back, will you? You dumb bitch. Get off it. You're on me all the time.

DONNA: I ain't.

PHIL (*heading toward* MICKEY's *room, he opens the door and looks in*): The fuck you ain't.

DONNA: I'm sorry. I'm just sittin' here.

PHIL: With your head up your ass.

DONNA (*she grabs up a magazine*): I was readin' a magazine.

PHIL (*coming down the stairs*): With your head up your ass.

DONNA: Boy, you are really an insulting form of person. Honest to God. Let a person have some rest.
(*On his way to the kitchen,* PHIL *freezes and then whirls to face her.*)

PHIL: Meaning me? (*He storms to the TV.*)

DONNA: Whata you mean?

PHIL (*turning off the TV*): I mean, "meaning me?" Who's SOMETHING?

DONNA: I didn't mean nothin'. I never mean nothin'.

PHIL: You said it though, didn't you?

DONNA: What?

PHIL (*rushing to the record player to turn it off*): What you said? You fuckin' said it.

DONNA: I don't know what you're talkin' about. Exactly.

PHIL (*heading into the kitchen where he starts to pour the popcorn in a bowl and tries to make sandwiches*): What I'm talkin' about is how you are and what you said. You

see a guy has undergone certain difficulties so his whole
appearance thing is a mood thing of how he is obviously
in a discouraged state, he's full of turmoil, does it occur
to you to say a kindly thing or to cut his fuckin' heart
out? You got your tongue out to sharpen your knife is
what you're up to, or do you want to give me some other
explanation?

DONNA: Sure, because—

PHIL (*rushing back to face her*): So what is it?

DONNA: WHAT?!

PHIL: YOUR SO-CALLED EXPLANATION! LET'S HEAR IT!

DONNA: I'M JUST— (*In exasperation, she is standing on the
couch.*)

PHIL: BULLSHIT! BULLSHIT!!!!!

DONNA: NOOOOOOOOO!!!

PHIL (*whirling to* EDDIE, *who has just stepped in the front
door with clothes from the cleaners*): Would you listen
to this airhead?

EDDIE: How's everything?

PHIL: Terrific. It's all totally fucked up, which I wouldn't have
it any other way. I thought you was here.

EDDIE: I hadda go out.

PHIL (*moving toward* EDDIE): Your car was here. What the
fuck is going on?

EDDIE: It wasn't far, so I walked. Donna, hey, I thought you were on your way to—

PHIL (*grabbing* EDDIE): Listen, Eddie! I saw the car, I thought you were here, you know, I was talkin' to you, you wasn't here, so I sounded like this asshole, so the ditz here has got to get on me about it.

EDDIE: Don't fuck with Phil, Donna.

DONNA: I wasn't, Eddie.

EDDIE: I mean, did you bring her, Phil?

PHIL: Who?

DONNA: No, no, no.

EDDIE: Her. Two hours ago, I was droppin' her at the freeway entrance.

DONNA: I was hitchhiking, Eddie, and it was like he come outa nowhere and it was, wow, Mickey. Whata hot car. So I set out for San Francisco like we talked about but I ended up here.

PHIL: I mean, what is it with this goddamn broad that makes her tick? I wanna know what makes her fuckin' tick. You answer me that goddamn question, will you?

DONNA: What?

PHIL: What makes you tick? I come here to see Eddie, you gotta be here. I wanna watch the football game and talk over some very important issues which pertain to my life, you gotta be here. What the fuck makes you tick?

DONNA: What's he talkin' about?

EDDIE: I don't know.

PHIL: What I'm talkin' about is—

EDDIE (*stepping in front of him as he moves toward* DONNA):
Listen, Phil, if Darlene comes by, you just introduce
Donna as your ditz, okay? (*He starts up the stairs for his
room.*)

DONNA: Who's Darlene, Phil?

PHIL (*his hands up in surrender, he retreats into the kitchen*):
I'm beggin' you. I'm beggin' you. I don't wanna see you,
okay? I don't wanna see you.

DONNA: Okay.

PHIL (*grabbing his beer and bowl of popcorn*): I mean, I come
in here and you gotta be here; I'm thinkin' about football, and you gotta be here with your tits and your ass
and this tight shrunken clothes and these shriveled
jeans, so that's all I'm thinking about from the minute I
see you is tits and ass. Football doesn't have a chance
against it. It's like this invasion of tits and ass overwhelming my own measly individuality so I don't have a
prayer to have my own thoughts about my own things
except you and tits and ass and sucking and fucking and
that's all I can think about. My privacy has been demol-
ished. (*Sitting down next to her on the couch. As he
talks, she nibbles his popcorn.*) You think a person wants
to have that kind of thing happen to their heads—they
are trying to give their own problems some serious
thought, the next thing they know there's nothing in
their brains as far as they can see but your tits and ass?
You think a person likes that?

DONNA: Who's playin'?

PHIL: You think a person likes that?

DONNA: No.

PHIL: Who's playin' what?

DONNA: Football.

PHIL: None of your fuckin' business.

DONNA: I like it.

PHIL: What are you talkin' about? I don't know what you're talkin' about!

DONNA: Football.

PHIL: You're nuts! (*Leaping up to run to the armchair and turn on the TV.*)

DONNA: I wanna watch it with you.

PHIL: You're nuts! You wanna watch the game? You're talkin' about you wanna watch the football game? Are you nuts? Are you crazy?

DONNA: What?

PHIL: How you gonna watch it? You don't know about it. You don't know nothing about it.

DONNA: I do. I know the points, and the insignias, and the—

PHIL: That's not the game.

DONNA (*she is leaping about the room now, demonstrating what she knows*): And when they go through the air and they catch it.

PHIL: Get outta here. I don't want you here.

DONNA: I know about the mascots. (*She sticks her head into his face.*)

PHIL: That's not the game. You don't know about the fucking game. Hut, hut, hut—

DONNA: I know about the—
    (*He butts his head into hers.*)

PHIL: That's the game. That's the game.

DONNA: Ohh, ouch ouch, awwwwww owwwwww.
    (EDDIE *comes out of his bedroom, a bunch of clothes in his hands.*)

EDDIE: What's this now?

PHIL: She's cryin'. What the fuck is the matter with her?

DONNA: He hit me, he hit me.

PHIL: She says she wants to know about the game.

EDDIE (*coming down the stairs*): What game?

DONNA: Football—

PHIL: —football! (*He turns off the TV.*)

DONNA: That's all.

PHIL: She's nuts.

DONNA (*as* EDDIE *examines her head*): He hit me. Am I bleedin'? Eddie, Eddie, Eddie.

EDDIE: No.

DONNA (*running to the record player, grabbing the record*): This is shit, this is shit. (*And she hits* EDDIE *with the album as she goes running by.*) This is shit.

EDDIE: What happened?

PHIL: I don't know. It was over too fast.

EDDIE: What?

PHIL: This thing here, whatever it was that happened here. She wanted to know about football, you know, the crazy bitch. She can't know about football. It's impossible. It's totally one hundred percent impossible. So this is what happens.
(*Going into the bathroom,* DONNA *slams the door.*)

So how you doin'?

EDDIE: Great. (*Heading back up the stairs.*) Me and Darlene are goin' to the desert.

PHIL: So guess what?

EDDIE: What?

PHIL (*heading up after* EDDIE): It's almost decided. I'm almost decided about going back to Susie.

EDDIE (*as* EDDIE *goes into his room*): What?

PHIL (*hovering outside* EDDIE's *room*): I can't stand it. The loneliness. And some form of totally unusual and unpredictable insanity is creeping up on me about to do I don't know WHAT—God forbid I find out. So I been thinkin' maybe if we had the kid, everything, or at least the main things, might be okay.

EDDIE (*coming out of his bedroom*): What kid?

PHIL: We were tryin' to have a kid. That's what we been doin'.

EDDIE: You and Susie?

PHIL: Eddie, wake up here! Who do you think? Yeah, me and Susie. She wants a kid. All her friends have been havin' 'em.

EDDIE (*as he moves along the balcony toward the bathroom door*): It's that goddamn age where it hits 'em like a truck, this maternal urge; they gotta have a kid—they don't know what hit 'em. (EDDIE *knocks on the bathroom door.*)

PHIL: The trouble is, though, what if it doesn't work out the way I planned?

EDDIE: Nothin' does, Phil.
(*As he knocks again, the bathroom door is flung open and* DONNA *storms out and into* MICKEY's *room, slamming shut that door.* EDDIE *steps into the bathroom, leaving* PHIL *hanging about, talking.*)

PHIL: I mean, I wanna have a kid sometimes, and sometimes I'm scared to death, and mostly though, I mean, for the last month or so it was like in my thoughts in my mind sometimes that this little baby had this big gun to my head and she would shoot me sooner or later.

EDDIE (*as* EDDIE *comes out of the bathroom, zipping up a shaving kit, and heading for his room*): So you don't want a kid.

PHIL: I do and I don't.

EDDIE (*pausing on the balcony, he faces* PHIL): I think this might be the thing here, you know, about which you two have been fighting so much lately. You shouldn't probably have one now. Just go back and get some, you know, clarity, so you both know what the issues are. This is the relationship I'm talkin' about. Straighten that out.

PHIL: Right. And then see. That makes sense.

EDDIE: Sure. (EDDIE *steps into his room.*)

PHIL: Except she has to have one.

EDDIE (*coming out of his room, carrying a small suitcase*): She doesn't have to have one.

PHIL (*following* EDDIE *as they descend the stairs*): I tried tellin' her that, because you know I got three kids, two little boys and a girl who are now, you know, I don't know how old, in Toledo, I haven't seen 'em since I went to prison. I don't want any more kids out there, you know, rollin' around their beds at night with this sick fucking hatred of me. I can't stand it.

EDDIE (*at the kitchen counter, he grabs his dope box and heads to the couch in order to pack it into the suitcase*): So don't have the kid now.

PHIL: Except she's desperate. I can't stand it when she cries.

EDDIE (*stopping on his way to the couch, he whirls on* PHIL):

You-can't-stand-it-when-she-cries is no reason to have a kid, Phil. I mean, there is involved here this totally innocent unborn human being totally dependent on your good will.

PHIL: It's fuckin' depressing. How about some weed? I want some weed.

EDDIE: What I'm sayin', Phil, is first things first.

PHIL: Like what?

EDDIE: The marriage; the marriage. (*Giving a joint to* PHIL. EDDIE *lights it for him and gives* PHIL *complete attention now as they settle onto the couch.*) I mean, no kid and a divorce is who-gives-a-fuck, but you have a kid and it's seismic. A big ten on the Richter scale. Carnage, man, that's what I'm sayin'. Gore on the highway, Phil.

PHIL: Right. Sure. (*Crossing away toward the hassock with the joint.*) Except, see, the trouble is, Susie has wanted to be a mother since she was twelve, you know. She had dolls and teddy bears and she dressed them up in diapers—you know—she still does it sometimes. This cute little bear.

EDDIE (*moving toward* PHIL): I mean, you're not thinkin' of going back and just, you know, hoping for the best; I mean, just trusting it to luck that she won't get pregnant. You're not thinkin' that.

PHIL: No, fuck, no.

EDDIE: Because you won't have a chance if you're sayin' that, and you go back. (*He crosses back to his suitcase.*)

PHIL: I got it covered. There's nothin' to worry about on that score. I been takin' this stuff and messing the whole thing up, which is why we ain't pregnant at this very minute.

EDDIE: Whata you mean?

PHIL: You know, my sperm count is monstrous on its own.

EDDIE: Whata you mean?

PHIL: I have a very high sperm count. It's record setting.

EDDIE: What stuff?

PHIL: Stuff. You know, it's harmful to the sperm and I'm messing myself up.

EDDIE: You're taking some kind of— Wait a minute! You're telling me you're taking some kind of poison?

PHIL: That's why I hadda talk to you, Eddie.

EDDIE (*advancing on* PHIL): You mean, insteada tellin' her what you want, you been taking some kind of goddamn poison. This is crazy, Phil! This is nuts! It's fucking nuts!

PHIL: It's not poison.

EDDIE: Listen to me! Do me a favor! Tell her what's been going on. You can tell her, can't you? I mean, don't you think maybe this is why the hell you two been fighting?

PHIL: Are you mad at me?

EDDIE: No.

PHIL: You're sure.

EDDIE: I'm just excited. Sometimes I get like I'm angry when I get excited. (*He crosses to the kitchen to pour himself a drink.*)

PHIL: Right. Because you are absolutely without a doubt one hundred percent right in everything you're saying, but if I don't do it, what's gonna happen?

EDDIE (*grabbing an unopened bottle of bourbon, he heads for the suitcase to pack the bottle*): Listen to me—are you a deaf man? Am I only under the delusion that I'm speaking? What you're telling me is a horror story—one part of you is begging another part to stop, but you don't hear you. But I do, I hear you—and you have got to stop, Phil.

PHIL: But what if I can't!

EDDIE: You gotta!

PHIL: Without a doubt. And I'm going to do it, I just want to know what kind of latitude I have regarding our friendship if my mind gets changed.

EDDIE: What'd she do, hypnotize you? Is this voodoo?

PHIL: No.

EDDIE: YOU'RE A GROWN MAN! You have asked me to tell you. I'm telling you: "TELL HER!"

PHIL: You're not answering my question. I'm talking about our friendship here!

EDDIE: Our friendship doesn't matter here. Our friendship is totally, categorically, one hundred percent irrelevant here. (*Turning to the suitcase, he tosses the bottle to the side of the couch, and works at straightening the suit-case.*)

PHIL: Eddie, listen to yourself! What are you saying? This is our friendship—this conversation—these very exchanges. We are in our friendship at this very moment. What could be more important?

EDDIE: I mean, I don't feel . . .
(*Grabbing* EDDIE *by the shoulders,* PHIL *forces* EDDIE *to square off with him face to face, eyeball to eyeball.*)

WHAT?

PHIL: Scorn. You feel scorn for me.

EDDIE: No.

PHIL: It's in your eyes.

EDDIE: No. What?

PHIL (*peering into* EDDIE's *eyes*): These dark thoughts, Eddie, I see them reflected in your eyes, they pertain to something other than me, or what?

EDDIE: I'm not having dark thoughts.

PHIL (*backing away*): Beyond the thoughts you're thinking, Eddie.

EDDIE (*he moves to unzip the shaving kit to get out a container of Alka-Seltzer as* PHIL *keeps following him*): No!

PHIL (*still backing away*): Then what the hell are you thinking about? I come for advice and you're off on some other totally unrelated tangent! (*As he spies the suitcase* EDDIE *has been carefully packing.)* Is that the thing here, the goddamn bottom line? I need your attention, and you're off in some fucking daydream? I'm desperate and you are, for crissake, distracted? *(As* EDDIE *has come running forward to save his things.)* Is this friendship, Eddie? Tell me!

EDDIE: Wait a minute.

PHIL: You want a fucking minute? *(Hurling* EDDIE *onto the couch,* PHIL *is on the verge of smashing his fist down on* EDDIE's *face. Recoiling,* EDDIE *covers up.)*

EDDIE: I don't know what you're talking about.

PHIL *(realizing what he is at the edge of doing,* PHIL *pulls back)*: Dark thoughts. Your dark thoughts, Eddie. This is not uncommon for people to have them. You were provoked; think nothing of it. But please—this, now—dark thoughts and everything included, this is our friendship. Pay attention to it, it's slipping by.

EDDIE: I wanna! YEAH, but I'm gettin' confused here, Phil. I tol' you—I don't feel good.

PHIL *(seeing the bottle that* EDDIE *didn't pack lying on the side of the couch, he grabs it)*: It's chaotic is why you're confused, Eddie. That's why you're confused. Think nothin' of it. I'm confused. *(Opening the bottle, he takes a drink.)* The goddamn situation is like this masked fucking robber come to steal the goods, but we don't even know is he, or isn't he. *(He hands* EDDIE *the open bottle.)* I mean, we got these dark thoughts, I see 'em in you, you don't think you're thinkin' 'em, so we can't even nail that down, how we going to get beyond it? They are the results of your unnoticed inner goings-on or my gigantic paranoia, both of which exist, so the goddamn thing in its entirety is on the basis of what has got to be called a coin toss.

EDDIE: I mean, you come here, you want advice, so I say do this; you say you can't; so I say try something else, but you can't—

PHIL: I'm sorry, Eddie.

EDDIE: I can figure it! You know I can, that's why you came to me. But I feel like you're drillin' little hunks a cottage cheese into my brain. Next thing, you're sayin', it's a goddamn coin toss—it's not a goddamn coin toss!

PHIL: You think I'm being cynical when I say that? Nothing is necessary, Eddie. Not a fucking thing! We're in the hands of something, it could kill us now or later, it don't care. Who is this guy that makes us just—you know— WHAT? (*Seeing the dictionary on the end table, he grabs it, starts leafing pages, looking wildly through it.*) THERE'S A NAME FOR THIS—IT HAPPENS— THERE'S A WORD FOR IT—EVERYBODY KNOWS IT. I CAN'T THINK OF IT. IT'S LIKE A LAW. IT IS A LAW. WHAT'S A LAW? WHAT THE FUCK IS A LAW?! (*He hurls the book onto the floor.*) Cynicism has nothing to do with it, Eddie, I've done my best. The fucking thing is without a clue, except the mess it leaves behind it, the guts and gore. (*Seeing the mess he made, he grabs the suitcase and starts to try to repack it, stuffing things back into it, but he can't. He stops.*) What I'm sayin' is, if my conclusion is contrary to your wishes, at least give me the fucking consideration and respect that you know that at least from my point of view it is based on solid thought and rock-hard evidence that has led me to I have no other choice, so you got no right to fuck with me about it. I want your respect.

EDDIE: You got that, Phil.

PHIL: I do?

EDDIE: Don't you know that?

PHIL: Sometimes I'm out in the rain, I don't even know it's rainin'. (*He paces away.*)

EDDIE: I'm just sayin'—all I'm sayin' is, "Don't have the baby thoughtlessly."

PHIL: Eddie, for godsake, don't terrify me that you have paid no attention! If I was thoughtless would I be here? (*Recoiling, he faces away, sitting on the hassock unable to look at* EDDIE, *who, on the couch, drinks, holding the bottle, pouring drinks into his glass and drinking. Or perhaps, neatly repacks the entire suitcase during this speech.*) I feel like I have pushed thought to the brink where it is just noise and of no more use than a headful of car horns, because the bottom line here that I'm getting at is just this—I got to go back to her. I got to go back to Susie, and if it means havin' a kid, I got to do it. I mean, I have hit a point where I am going round the bend several times a day now, and so far I been on the other side to meet me, but one a these times might be one too many, and what then? I'm a person, Eddie, and I have realized it, who needs like a big-dot-thing, you know—this big-dot-thing around which I can just hang and blab my thoughts and more or less formulate everything as I go, myself included. I mean, I used to spend my days in my car; I didn't know what the fuck I was doin' but it kept me out of trouble until nothin' but blind luck led me to I-am-married, and I could go home. She was my big-dot-thing. Now I'm startin' in my car again, I'm spendin' days on the freeways. Rain or no rain I like the wipers

clickin', and all around me the other cars got people in 'em the way I see 'em when they are in cars. These heads, these faces. These boxes of steel with glass and faces inside. I been the last two whole days and nights without seeing another form of human being in his entirety except gas station attendants. The freeways, the cloverleafs got a thing in them sometimes it spins me off, I go where I never meant to. There's little back roads and little towns I never heard of them. I start to expect the gas station attendants to know me when I arrive. I get excited that I've been there before. I want them to welcome me. I'm disappointed when they don't.
(*Faintly, the music starts, the music from the beginning, the theme, the harmonica loop from "Unchained Melody."*)

Something that I don't want to be true starts lookin' like it's all that's true only I don't know what it is. No. No. I need my marriage. I come here to tell you. I got to stay married. I'm lost without her.
(*The door to* MICKEY's *room slams as* DONNA *bursts out.* PHIL, *startled, stands up, looking up at her.* EDDIE *is also looking up. She is dressed as she arrived, in her traveling clothes. She carries her knapsack and record. She stomps down the stairs to the landing, then faces them.*)

DONNA: You guys have cooked your goose. You can just walk your own dog, and fuck yourselves. These particular tits and ass are taking a hike. (*With the music building, she stomps to the door, opens it, turns, looks at* EDDIE, *who is staring at her, quite ill.*) So this is goodbye. (*She goes out, slamming the door.* EDDIE *and* PHIL *stare after her, unmoving.*)

CURTAIN

ACT TWO

Time: Night. A year later.

Place: The same.

EDDIE, *wearing his glasses, sits on the couch reading a script, a glass containing ice and bourbon in his hand. The door opens and* PHIL *comes in followed by* ARTIE. *They are very excited, rushing in; they are high from what has happened, laughing, giddy.*

PHIL: This guy, what a fuckin' guy.

ARTIE: You shoulda seen him. He was unbelievable.

EDDIE: So what happened?
(*As, above them,* MICKEY, *wearing slacks but no shirt, appears in the doorway to his room, talking on the phone, a drink in his hand.*)

PHIL: I decked him. He deserved it.

EDDIE: Who?
(MICKEY *steps back into his room.*)

85

PHIL (*rushing to the refrigerator to get a beer*): Some punk—he made me mad.

EDDIE: So you decked some guy.

ARTIE (*getting in* EDDIE's *way as* EDDIE *tries to move to* PHIL): You shoulda seen it. He went across the room like he was on wheels.

EDDIE: So what'd he do?

ARTIE (*as* MICKEY, *pulling on a fashionable T-shirt, reappears above them*): He was a jerk.

EDDIE: I mean why'd you hit him? (*Heading to the counter behind which* PHIL *stands.*)

PHIL: He got up! (*This is outrageous, and he includes* MICKEY *in the joke as* MICKEY, *leaning on the railing, looks down.*)

EDDIE: I mean, before he got knocked down—the first time you hit him, why'd you hit him?

ARTIE (*again, he jumps in front of* EDDIE): You wouldn't believe this guy. He was genuinely irritating.

PHIL: This is the pitiful part. I don't think he could help himself.

ARTIE (*rushing to* PHIL): I mean, this is the way this pathetic jerk-off must go through his life. IRRITATING!

PHIL (*to* ARTIE, *laughing*): It's a curse to be this guy! I shoulda had some consideration.

EDDIE: BUT WHAT HAPPENED?

ARTIE: He was sayin' this unbelievable dumb stuff to this broad.

EDDIE (*in the kitchen* EDDIE *pours another drink*): Some broad you knew?

ARTIE: Noooo! (*As if this is the dumbest question anybody ever could have asked. And then again he gets his nose in* PHIL's *face as they share the absurdity of this guy.*) Just this genuinely repulsive broad.

PHIL (*to* ARTIE, *laughing, hugging* ARTIE): And he's talkin' to her like she's somethin' gorgeous. THIS DOG! It was offensive.

ARTIE: Very irritating guy, this guy.

EDDIE: I can see that.

PHIL: You shoulda been there. (*Moving out around the counter closer to* EDDIE *as* ARTIE *trails along behind* PHIL.) I ask him to shut up, and he says he isn't botherin' anybody. I say he is botherin' me; he looks at me like I'm an asshole; I can see he's askin' for it. (*Turning to* ARTIE *and laughing.*) So I warn him one more time.

EDDIE: What'd you say?

PHIL: I don't SAY nothing. I look at him very seriously, you know, bullets and razors and bloodshed in my eyes, but all under control, so he can have the option of knowing nothing need happen if he don't push me. But he's gotta push me, I gotta deck the guy.

MICKEY: So what happened?

PHIL: HE GETS UP!

MICKEY: He gets up? This is unbelievable. You knock him down, and he gets up?

ARTIE: Phil don't just knock him down. He knocks him across the room. (*And now* ARTIE *glides backward into the banister that supports the landing.*) It's like this goddamn vortex just snarfs him up and fucking magnetizes him to the wall for a full second before he slides to the floor. SO THEN HE GETS UP! Do you believe this guy?

MICKEY: This is some tough guy, huh?

ARTIE *and* PHIL: NOOOOO! (*As if this is an insanely stupid question.*)

PHIL: Absolutely not. (*Crossing to the coat hook on the support beam near the front door, he hangs his jacket.* ARTIE, *following closely to hang his own jacket on the hooks on the closet door.*) This is a weak link on the chain of humanity other than in his particular capacities of irritating; and this is where the real irony comes in. Because I don't think, looking back, that when he got up on his feet again he any longer had a clue to where he was or what he was doin'.

ARTIE: He was totally fuckin' unconscious.

PHIL: Exactly. Looking back, I can see he was no longer from his point of view in the bar even. From his point of view he was on his way to catch a bus or something.

ARTIE: It was his reflexes.

PHIL (*while* ARTIE, *still excited, is explaining to* MICKEY *and* EDDIE, PHIL *is slowly becoming downcast*): Exactly, but I don't see he's harmless in time to take charge of my own reflexes, which see nothing at all except that he's comin' toward me. So I gotta let him have it. It's him or me.

ARTIE: But as far as attacking Phil, it's the farthest thing from his mind.

PHIL: No, he's like going shopping or something. He don't know what he's doing. It's just his reflexes.

ARTIE: So Phil's reflexes got the best of him.

PHIL: So we are both victims of our reflexes.

MICKEY (*pronouncing from on high*): So, this is a tragedy here.

PHIL (*pacing away from* ARTIE *downstage of the couch*): I don't know that, but it was a mess, and I coulda got into real trouble, because the second time the whack I put on him was beyond the realm of normal human punches.
(ARTIE, *seeing that* PHIL's *mood is changing, is approaching him from behind, moving in* PHIL's *wake around the couch.*)

That he didn't disintegrate was both his and my good fortune.

ARTIE: Don't get morose, Phil, huh? (*Patting* PHIL, *trying to cheer him up.*) Pay attention to the upside.

PHIL: You pay attention to the upside—you're the big deal— I'm the fuck-up. (*Pulling away,* PHIL *moves to the kitchen counter for something to drink.*)

EDDIE (EDDIE *is sitting there on one of the stools, a drink in his hand. He has been there all along, watching as* PHIL *and* ARTIE *spun off*): You let off some steam, Phil. This is the purpose of this kind of, you know, out and out bullshit.

PHIL (*behind the counter, leaning on the bar like a drunk in a tavern*): You wanna tell me how come I have all the necessary realizations that any normal human being might have—only by the time I have them, nothin' but blind luck has saved me from doin' a lifetime in the can, and they can serve no possible purpose but to torment me with the realization that I am a totally out-of-control prick!?

ARTIE: Phil has got violent karma, that's all; it's in the cards. (*Settling down on the couch, he has a notebook in which he scribbles.*)

PHIL: Yeah, well, if this is my karma, fuck it.

MICKEY: (*moving to descend the stairs*): Absolutely, right; fuck destiny, fate and all metaphysical stuff.

PHIL (*bolting to the base of the stairway where he glares up at* MICKEY): You, you cynical bastard, watch the fine line you are walking between my self-awareness and my habitual trend to violence. 'Cause on the one hand I might appear worried, but on the other I could give a fuck, you know, and my urge to annihilate anyone might just fixate on you.

MICKEY (*pausing on the stairs*): And the vortex get me—fling me, you might say, wallward, magnetically.

PHIL: Exactly. So you can help us both out by watching your goddamn, you know. Right? Am I making myself clear?

MICKEY (*slipping by* PHIL): Step.

PHIL: Yeah. P's and Q's. (*Moving after* MICKEY, *who glides straight down to sit in the swivel chair, picking up a* Variety *that sits there;* PHIL *veers off, heading to* ARTIE, *who is on the couch.*) So, Artie, you got any inside dope on this karma thing, or you just ranting?

ARTIE: Everybody knows something, it's a popular topic.

PHIL: But what I'm asking you is, "You said it, do you know it?"

EDDIE (*from the bar where he still sits, growing a little irritated that* PHIL *is so uninterested in what he has to say on things*): I mean, Phil, isn't the fact of the matter here that you signed your divorce papers today?

PHIL: Who said anything about that? One thing does not lead to another.

EDDIE: I mean, I think that's what you're wired up about.

PHIL: Eddie, you're jumpin' around on me, here, what's your point?

EDDIE: The baby, the baby. The divorce. This is the ambush you been worried about. They got you. They blew you RIGHT the fuck out of orbit, and if you see maybe that's what's cooking under the whole thing, you might just get a hold of yourself.

MICKEY: And pull yourself back into orbit.

PHIL: But what orbit? I'm in an orbit.

MICKEY (*in the chair, his back to* PHIL, *he tosses the remark over his shoulder*): It's just it's a useless fucking orbit.

PHIL (*advancing on* MICKEY, *who sits, his attention on the paper*): Do you know, Mickey, I could kick your eyes out and never think about it a second time, that's the depths to which my animosity runs?!

MICKEY: I know that.

PHIL: So why do you take these chances and risk ruining both our lives?

MICKEY (*standing, he faces* PHIL *and points to* ARTIE *on the couch*): This is the very point Artie was, I think, making.

PHIL: Artie, is this your point? (*Turning to* ARTIE, *as* MICKEY *crosses toward the bar for ice and more to drink, and there sits* EDDIE.)

ARTIE: What? (ARTIE *does not even look up from his scribbling, as* PHIL *hastens to join him.*)

PHIL: Is this your point?

ARTIE: What?

EDDIE: Mickey! Will you just cut the goofy shit for a second? This is a serious point I'm trying to make here.

MICKEY: He knows his life is a mess.

EDDIE: He doesn't know it enough.

MICKEY: He knows it so goddamn well he's trying to avoid it.

EDDIE: That's my point! (*Whirling to cross to* PHIL.) I mean, Phil, if you see the goddamn issue here. PHIL!

Phil (*looking up from* Artie's *endeavor*): YEAH. What's Artie doin'?

Artie: I had a thought.

Phil (*as he moves to follow* Eddie, *who has crossed up near the record player as if seeking privacy*): So you wrote it down? Everybody has a thought, Artie, this is no justification they go around writing them down.

Eddie: You're just on a goddamn wild roll here because of the state of your life being a shambles! The baby's born and you sign the divorce papers all in the same month, so you're under stress.

Phil: I'm aware of that.

Eddie: So that's what I'm sayin'. See the connection.

Phil: But why are you trying to torment me, Eddie? I thought I could count on you. (*He keeps watching* Artie, *who appears to be listening to their conversation and then taking notes on what he hears.*)

Eddie: But lighten up is what I'm saying, give yourself a break. I mean, the real issues are not you hitting people or not hitting people but are these other issues of your divorce and baby. You enjoy hitting people and you know it.

Phil: My point is not that I don't enjoy it but that it is dangerous (*as* Artie, *looking at his watch, heads to the phone in the kitchen nook,* Phil *looks after him*), even if what Artie says is right, which I don't understand it, but I would like to. Because my point is that I am wired beyond my reasons. I know my reasons, but I am wired beyond them. (*As he heads toward* Artie *in the kitchen, he meets* MICKEY, *moving in the opposite direction, of-fering him a joint, his manner very friendly.*)

MICKEY: You're right on schedule, Phil, that's all. You're a perfectly, rapateta, blah-blah-blah, modern statistic; you have the baby, you get the divorce. You're very "now" is all, but not up to it. You're the definitive representative of the modern male in this year, but you're not willing to accept it. (*Moving onto the couch.*)

PHIL: This is what I gotta talk to Artie about. (*He rushes to* ARTIE, *seated outside the L of the nook, the phone in his hand, a message beeper pressed to the phone.*) Artie, what the fuck are you doing?

ARTIE: I'm checking my messages. (*He beeps the beeper.*)

PHIL (*pacing behind the counter but trying to be nice, trying to be patient, and a little funny, charming, he hopes*): You got a minute, this is a disaster here. I'm on the brink and you're checking your fucking messages. Have some compassion.

ARTIE: Just a second. (*As he listens to his messages.*)

EDDIE (EDDIE, *crossing from the record player where* PHIL *left him, moves at* ARTIE): So who'd you hear from, huh? You got studio executives lined up on your goddamn machine beep after beep. (*Mimicking different voices.*) "Great project, Arthur." "Terrific treatment." "Must have lunch."

ARTIE: I have a career. I am not ashamed, I have a career. You want me to be ashamed?

EDDIE (*face to face with* ARTIE, *he pours himself a drink*): What I want you to understand, Artie, is the absurdity of this business, and the fact that you're a success in it is a measure of the goddamn absurdity of this business . . . (*finished pouring his drink, he moves off toward the couch where* MICKEY *sits*) . . . to which we are all desperate to belong as a bunch of dogs.

ARTIE: You're a small-minded prick, Eddie; I hope you know that.

MICKEY: He does.

EDDIE (*settling with his drink and bottle onto the couch*): I am familiar with the opinion. However, I do not myself hold it.

PHIL (*unable to wait any longer, he grabs at the phone, but* ARTIE *eludes him*): But what I need, Artie, is a little more, you know what I mean, Artie. What I'm wondering here is, you got any particularly useful, I mean, hard data on this karma stuff, you know, the procedures by which this cosmic shit comes down. That's what I'm asking: Do you know what you're talking about?

MICKEY: He's a Jew.

PHIL (*moving out to put his arm around* ARTIE): I know he's a Jew. I'm talking to him, ain't I? Destiny is a thing you have to be somewhat educated to have a hint about it, so he might know somebody, right, Artie? You know anybody?

EDDIE: But it's another tradition, Phil.

PHIL: Who gives a fuck! (*He comes storming out at them.*) Of course I know that. But I'm not talking about tradition here—I'm asking him about the cosmos and has he come upon anything in all the fucking books he reads that might tell me more than I pick up off the TV which is, strictly speaking, dipshit.

ARTIE (*behind* PHIL, *hanging up the phone*): Sure.

PHIL (*whirling to face* ARTIE, *who is pulling a book from his pocket*): See. So what is it?

ARTIE: Hey, you know, past lives. (*Stepping up, the book open to a marker, he hands the book to* PHIL, *who settles on the stool to read.*) You have past lives and the karmic stuff accrues to it. You have debits and credits and you have to work your way out from under the whole thing, so you—

MICKEY: Artie! This is not your investment counselor we're talking about here.

EDDIE: This is not cosmic Visa, Artie.
   (MICKEY *and* EDDIE *are both mocking* ARTIE *now*— MICKEY, *wanting to keep* PHIL *from being taken seriously by anyone, and* EDDIE *because he is irritated that* PHIL *seems more interested in* ARTIE'S *opinions than in the advice* EDDIE *himself has tried to give.*)

ARTIE: We could be in the process of working out the debits and credits of our past lives with the very way we relate to each other at this very instant. (*Stepping toward* MICKEY *and* EDDIE.) It could be that Phil owes some affection to me, I owe him some guidance, and—

EDDIE (*laughing even more now,* MICKEY *and* EDDIE *both breaking up*): Guidance?

MICKEY: The fact that you're talking, Artie, does not necessarily make it destiny speaking, I hope you know this.

ARTIE (*irritated,* ARTIE *retreats toward his student and friend of the evening,* PHIL): And you two pricks owe some negative shit to everybody.

PHIL: Artie, he's right. (*Disappointed to have been given a book, and seeing the ridicule that* MICKEY *and* EDDIE *bear the subject,* PHIL *wants no part of it, so he hands the book back to* ARTIE.) You make it sound like the cosmos is in your opinion this loan shark. This is disappointing.

ARTIE: You asked me.

PHIL: Because I thought you might know.
(*Angrily,* ARTIE *flops down in the armchair, turning his back on them all.*)

MICKEY (*moving past* ARTIE *on his way to the bar, he mocks* ARTIE): That's the TV fucking version, and don't you pretend you learned that anywhere but on the evening news.

EDDIE: Some goddamn Special Project.

PHIL (*at the bar with* MICKEY *now,* PHIL *tries to justify how he ended up almost taking such a ridiculous thing as karma seriously*): I was hoping, you know, he's a Jew. He's got this insane religious history running out behind him, he might have picked up something, you know. That's what I was hoping. (*Moving up behind* ARTIE, *he plays with* ARTIE's *hair.*) There might be some crazed Hasidic motherfucker in his family; you know, he came to dinner, he had his pigtail, nobody could shut him up about karma, destiny, the way of the stars; (*on his way to join* EDDIE *on the couch to make clear his allegiances*) it might have rubbed off on Artie.

MICKEY: You disappointed him, Artie. You built him up, you disappointed him.

ARTIE: It happens.

MICKEY: He's at a critical juncture in his life, here.

ARTIE: Who isn't?

EDDIE: You guys need to get laid.

MICKEY: You, however, don't, huh?

EDDIE: I am, in fact, sustaining a meaningful relationship.

ARTIE (*irritated that* EDDIE *and* MICKEY *have teased him, that* PHIL *has betrayed and teased him, he snaps at* EDDIE): The only thing sustaining that relationship is the fact that she's out of town two out of every three weeks.

EDDIE (*glaring at* ARTIE): Well, she's in town tomorrow.

MICKEY (*after an uneasy second, he smiles*): I wouldn't mind getting laid. What are we thinking about?

EDDIE: We could call somebody.

PHIL: Do it.

ARTIE: Do it now!

EDDIE: I was thinking primarily of setting Phil up, that's what I meant, primarily.

ARTIE: What about me?

EDDIE: Give me a break, Artie. Phil is in a totally unique

situation, here, back out in the single life. (*Patting* PHIL, *who sits beside him.*)

PHIL: I'm in a totally fucked-up state of mind, too.

EDDIE: So . . . (*on his way to the phone, he says pointedly to* ARTIE:) . . . I could call Bonnie.

ARTIE: You're not going to get Bonnie for Phil? (*Rushing in protest after* EDDIE.)

PHIL: I don't believe this treachery. Artie, have some mercy.

ARTIE (*whirling back to* PHIL *on the couch*): This is sex we're talking about now, Phil. Competitive sex.

PHIL: That's what I'm saying. I need help.

ARTIE: You're such a jerk-off, you're such a goof-off. (*He yells to* MICKEY:) He's got this thing.

PHIL: Relent, I beg you—I am feeling suicidal. Have I not explained myself?

ARTIE: I don't believe for a second you were seriously desperate about trying to pick that bitch up.

PHIL: That's exactly how out of touch I am, Artie—I have methods so outdated they appear to you a goof.

ARTIE (ARTIE *runs toward* MICKEY, *who has been watching from a stool at the counter;* EDDIE *is at the stage left end of the counter with the phone*): Fuck you. He's got this thing.

PHIL: Styles have changed. Did you see the look of disgust on that bimbo's excuse for a face? It was humiliating.

ARTIE (*trying to tell* MICKEY): He's got this thing!

MICKEY: What thing?
   (EDDIE *is at the phone, dialing.*)

PHIL: It used to work.

MICKEY: What?

PHIL: It's a vibrator that I carry around, see.

MICKEY: You carry around a vibrator with you?

PHIL: As a form of come-on, so they see I'm up for anything
   right from the get-go. It's very logical if you think about
   it. But tonight there were extenuating circumstances.

ARTIE: It's a logic apparent to you alone, Phil.

EDDIE (*slamming down the phone*): Bonnie, get off the fucking phone!

MICKEY (*to* EDDIE): He had a vibrator.

PHIL: I had a vibrator. So what?

EDDIE: It's logical.

PHIL: Right. Eddie understands me, thank God for it. So
   when I'm coming on to the broad, see, I sort of pull it
   out, and have it there. It's like some other guy might
   have a nail file or something only I got a vibrator. (*He
   hopes the subject is closed.*) So this Bonnie's a terrific
   broad, huh?

EDDIE: Terrific.

ARTIE: So you got your thing, Phil!

PHIL: So I'm delivering my pitch, you know, and we can have
a good time if we get an opportunity to be alone, and as a
kind of mood-setter, I turn it on, you know. Except I
forgot about the goddamn weights.
(ARTIE *laughs;* MICKEY *looks at* EDDIE *to see if he understands.*)

EDDIE: What?

MICKEY: THE WEIGHTS? YOU FORGOT ABOUT THE
WEIGHTS?

PHIL: I forgot about 'em. Unbelievable!

MICKEY: UNBELIEVABLE! YOU FORGOT ABOUT THE
WEIGHTS! (*Crossing to* PHIL *on the couch.*) HE FOR-
GOT ABOUT THE GODDAMN WEIGHTS!

ARTIE (*from the counter*): Do you know what he's talking
about?

MICKEY: No, I don't know what he's talking about!

PHIL (*leaping up to separate himself from* MICKEY, *who is on
the arm of the couch*): You prick. You disgust me. I'm
talking about the weights.

ARTIE (*running to* MICKEY): See, he has been transporting his
barbells and weights in the back of the car, with all his
inability to know where he lived.

PHIL (*starting toward* EDDIE): So the weights were in the back
of the car.

MICKEY: Right.

Phil: The train of events in this thing is perfectly logical to anybody with half a heart to see them, unless that person is a nasty prick. So what had to happen, happened, and I threw the weights into the trunk of the car carelessly and hit the vibrator without thinking about it.

Eddie: So you pulled out a broken vibrator on this broad.

Phil: Exactly.

Eddie: This is an emergency. I think this is an emergency situation here. (*Whirling back to the phone, he begins furiously dialing.*)

Phil: This is what I'm trying to tell you.

Eddie: You're a desperate human being, Phil.

Phil: I'm begging. Get Bonnie! I got this broken vibrator, and so when I turn it on, it goes round sort of all weird like, you know, and the motor's demented sounding, it's going around all crooked and weird, changing speeds. She's looking at me.

Eddie (*dialing again and again*): This really happened to you?

Phil: What can I do, Eddie? Help me.

Eddie: I'm trying.

Phil: So this broad is looking at me. She's givin' me this look. This thing's in my hand, arrrggghhh, like I'm offering to put this goddamn model airplane inside her. It's liable to come apart and throw her across the room.

Eddie: Bonnie, please. (*He slams down the phone.*)

ARTIE: This thing's goin', arrrggghhh, arrrghhh. Phil's sayin',
"Want to come home with me?"

PHIL: Arrghhhhh, arghhh, want to come home with me?
(EDDIE, *on the stool by the phone, stares at* PHIL.)

EDDIE: You really did this, Phil?

PHIL: Yeah.

EDDIE: Listen to me. You're a rare human being.

PHIL (*very pleased, swiveling the chair to face* EDDIE): So how
come everything turns to shit?

EDDIE: I don't know, but we're going to find out. You're a rare,
precious human being. (*Moving, he sits on the hassock;
they huddle face to face.*)

PHIL: I suspected as much.
(*Behind* PHIL, MICKEY *watches while* ARTIE, *after a moment, dozes.*)

EDDIE: Underneath all this bullshit, you have a real instinc-
tive thing, you know what I mean. It's like this wide-
open intuition.

PHIL: This is what I think sometimes about myself.

EDDIE: I mean, it's unique; this goddamn imagination—you
could channel it.

PHIL: I have thoughts sometimes they could break my head
open.

EDDIE: Whata you mean?

PHIL: I mean, these big thoughts. These big goddamn thoughts. I don't know what to do with them.

EDDIE: This is what I'm saying: if you could channel them into your talent. I mean, under all this crazed bullshit you've been forced to develop—

PHIL: I get desperate. I feel like my thoughts are all just going to burst out of my head and leave me; they're going to pick me up and throw me around the room. I fight with them. It's a bloodbath this monster I have with my thoughts. Maybe if I channeled them.

EDDIE: I never took you so seriously before. I mean quite so seriously.

PHIL: Me neither.

EDDIE (*he runs to the phone,* PHIL *right behind him*): I'm calling Bonnie, Phil. I'm calling her for you.

PHIL: So call her! (*As* EDDIE *grabs the phone,* PHIL *hugs* EDDIE *from behind, laying his chest on* EDDIE'*s back as* EDDIE *leans over the counter with the phone.*) Call her, call her, call her.

MICKEY (*staring at* EDDIE *and* PHIL, *he nudges* ARTIE): Could this be it, Artie?

ARTIE: What? (*Waking up.*)

MICKEY: Could this be destiny in fact at work, Artie, and we are witnessing it? The pattern in the randomness, so that we see it: man without a home, careless weights; broken vibrator, disappointed broad. And from this apparent mess . . . (*he gestures toward* EDDIE *and* PHIL *in their embrace;* ARTIE *follows the gesture to see* EDDIE *and* PHIL) . . . two guys fall in love.

EDDIE: He's jealous, Phil, don't worry about his petty jealousy.

PHIL: He could choke on his own spit, I would feel nothing. No. I would feel glee. I would be a kid at an amusement park. (*As* EDDIE *hangs up the phone, they maintain their embrace.*) She's still busy?

EDDIE: I'm gonna get her for you, Phil, don't worry.

PHIL: So who is this bitch she's on the phone forever, some goddamn agent?

EDDIE: No, no, she's terrific, you're gonna love her. This is a bitch who dances naked artistically in this club. That's her trip.

MICKEY: With a balloon.
(*Now they break apart.*)

EDDIE: That's what makes it artistic. Without the balloon, what is she?

ARTIE: A naked bitch.

EDDIE: You would wanna fuck her, though.

ARTIE: Anybody would.

EDDIE: She's a good bitch, though, you know what I mean? She's got a heart of gold.

MICKEY: What's artistic about her is her blow jobs.

PHIL (*grabbing the phone, he puts it to* EDDIE's *ear*): Get her, Eddie; get her.

MICKEY: She's critically acclaimed.

EDDIE (*dialing*): And the best part about her is that she's up for anything.

MICKEY: Like the airport. (*Crossing to the stage right edge of the counter for more to drink.*)

EDDIE: What airport? (*Then he screams into the phone:*) Bonnie, please!

MICKEY: So we ask her to go to the airport.

EDDIE: Oh Jesus, the airport!
(EDDIE, *the phone still in his hand, moves to* MICKEY *as the story, the claims of old times, the competitiveness of telling the story draw* MICKEY *and* EDDIE *into a teamlike intimacy, leaving* PHIL *watching from the far stage left stool while* ARTIE *watches from the couch.*)

MICKEY: This was amazing. Robbie Rattigan was coming in.

EDDIE: He was coming in, see, he was up for this major part in this pilot for an ABC series. Right? He's flying in, we wanna make him feel welcome.

MICKEY: He's gonna be all screwed up from the flight, he's got this big meeting.

EDDIE: Bonnie jumps at the chance. She's seen him as a featured killer on several cop shows which he was on almost every one of them as a killer.
(*That Rattigan played killers is an important bit of information, since that's what* PHIL *tends to play.*)

"Meet him at the airport," we tell her.

MICKEY: "He's a friend of ours," we tell her. "We want you to relax him on the drive back to town."

EDDIE: She says to us that she has been very impressed by his work when she saw it.

MICKEY: She's a fuckin' critic.

EDDIE: So we meet the plane. Robbie gets off, you know; we meet him, we get in the car. Hey, hey, blah-blah, blah-blah-blah. We're on the freeway, she's in the back seat with Robbie.
(EDDIE *and* MICKEY *have met now upstage near the railing and landing.*)

MICKEY: She's just there.

EDDIE: We made a point of just introducing her like she's somebody's girlfriend, you know, or just some bitch we know, she happens to be in the back seat when we pick him up.

MICKEY: An accident.

EDDIE: No big deal.

MICKEY: So Robbie's talkin' about the part he's up for, and getting very serious, "rapateta." So Bonnie reaches over and unzips his fly. He looks at her like she just fell out of a tree. "Don't mind me," she says.

EDDIE: I'm tellin' him to keep on talkin'.

MICKEY: We're acting like we don't know what's goin' on.

EDDIE: She just had this impulse. He's irresistible.

MICKEY: That's the impression.

EDDIE: That he's this irresistible guy. That's the impression
we want to make.

MICKEY: So she's gone down on him.

EDDIE: You can tell by his face.

MICKEY: She's very energetic.

EDDIE (*dialing one more time*): So he starts to curse us out.
You would not believe the cursing he does.

MICKEY: "Robbie," I tell him, "Welcome to L.A.!" (*Heading
for the armchair.*)

EDDIE (*into the phone*): Bonnie! Hello!
(*Everybody freezes.*)

Hello. Hey. Bonnie. Eddie. Yeah. C'mon over. Yeah.
C'mon over. (*He hangs up.*) She's comin' over.
(MICKEY *moves to the armchair and sits, leaving* EDDIE
up by the counter with PHIL.)

PHIL: She's comin' over? She's really comin'?

EDDIE: Yeah. Oh, the look on Robbie's face, and the look on
the kid's face. Remember that?

MICKEY: No. What?

EDDIE: The kid. Oh, yeah. Christ, the kid. She's got a six-year-
old daughter, and she was there.

MICKEY: She was with us?

EDDIE: In the front seat. I forgot about the kid. Wasn't she there?

MICKEY: Yeah. Remember?

EDDIE: Yeah.

MICKEY: So Robbie's wong comes out, and he's got one. I mean, this guy is epic.

EDDIE: Monstrous. The kid is petrified.

MICKEY: I mean, there's her mother goin' into combat with this horse.

EDDIE: It's a goddamn snake.

MICKEY: This is sick, isn't it? I'm gettin' a little sick.

EDDIE: We were ripped, though, weren't we? We were ripped.

MICKEY: Maybe we were blotto.

EDDIE (*moving in on* MICKEY): Then we woulda forgot the whole thing. Which we didn't.

MICKEY: We nearly did. I mean, about the kid, right?

EDDIE: I don't think the mitigating circumstances are sufficient! I ended up takin' care of her. She started to cry, remember?

MICKEY: No.

EDDIE: Sure. I mean, she didn't start to cry, but she looked

like somebody whacked her in the back of the head with
a rock. So I hadda take care of her. You remember,
Mickey!

Mickey: Almost. (*He turns away, a* Hollywood Reporter *in
his hands.*) I was drivin'. So then what happened? I was
personally blotto.

Eddie: Bullshit! (Eddie *faces him. He is not going to let*
Mickey *escape this one. He is going to make him remember.*) We ended up, I'm holdin' her, we're tellin' her
these goddamn stories, remember. She was there. We
were makin' up this story about elves and shit, and this
kingdom full of wild rabbits, and the elves were getting
stomped to death by gangs of wild rabbits.

Mickey: Jungle Bunnies, I think, is what we called them.

Eddie: Fuck. (*Finding more than he anticipated, he collapses
onto the hassock beside the chair on which* Mickey *sits.*)
Everywhere I turn I gotta face my own depravity. Jungle
Bunnies are stomping elves to death so the elves start to
hang them. Is that the story?

Mickey: Yeah. And we were doin' the voices.
(*Now they no longer know whether it was funny or
horrible.*)

Eddie: I don't wanna think about it. High-pitched, right?

Mickey: Yeah, high-pitched . . .

Mickey and Eddie: And rural!

Eddie: The kid was catatonic. I think maybe that was it,
Mickey; we turned the corner in this venture.

MICKEY: Right. What venture?

EDDIE: Life. That was the nosedive. I mean, where it began. We veered at that moment into utter irredeemable depravity.

MICKEY: I feel sick to my stomach about myself. A little. That I could do that. How could I do that?

PHIL: Hey. You guys. (*Advancing from the counter to where they sit drooping on the chair and hassock.*) Don't get crazy! You had a WHIM. This is what happens to people. THEY HAVE WHIMS. So you're sittin' around, Robbie's comin'. You want him to like you, you want him to think well of you. So you have this whim. Did she have to do it? Did anybody twist her arm?
(MICKEY *and* EDDIE *have straightened slowly.*)

MICKEY: Phil's right, Eddie. (*He gets to his feet.*) What'd we do? I mean, objectively. Did anybody say, "Bring your kid"? (*Off* MICKEY *walks, headed for the stairs.*)

EDDIE: It's the airwaves.

MICKEY: Exactly. (*Climbing the stairs.*)

EDDIE: TV. TV. (*He is staring at the television set. Now he stalks it, staring at it intently.* ARTIE *has sagged into a lying position on the couch, and* PHIL *is sinking into the armchair, as* MICKEY *climbs the stairs.* EDDIE, *talking to the TV:*) Once it was a guy from TV, what chance did she have? She couldn't help herself. And I think subconsciously we knew this. (*Whirling to call to* MICKEY, *climbing the stairs:*) Didn't we know it, Mickey? I mean, what does she watch? About a million hours of TV a week, so the airwaves are all mixed with the TV waves and then the whole thing is scrambled in her brain waves

so, you know, her head is just full of this static, this fog of
TV thoughts, to which she refers for everything. I mean
this is an opportunity to mix with the gods we're offering her in the back seat of our car.
(*The door opens and in comes* BONNIE.)

BONNIE: Hi!

EDDIE (*rushing to her*): Bonnie.

ARTIE: Hi!

BONNIE: Hi, Artie.

MICKEY: Hi. (*Having paused to wave at the top of the stairs,
he goes into the bathroom.*)

BONNIE: Hi, Mickey.
(EDDIE *is guiding her straight to* PHIL, *who sits in the
armchair.*)

Your call was a miracle, Eddie.

EDDIE: This is Phil.

BONNIE: Hi.

PHIL: Hi.

EDDIE: He's recently divorced.

BONNIE: Everybody I know is either recently married or recently divorced, some of them the same people. It's a
social epidemic.

PHIL: I'm recently divorced.

BONNIE: I've got to have some blow, Eddie, can you spare it?

EDDIE: Sure, hey.
(*They move to the counter.*)

BONNIE: Doom and gloom have come to sit in my household like some permanent kind of domestic appliance. My brain has been invaded with glop.
(PHIL *is drifting from the chair to lurk behind her.*)

If you could spare some blow to vacuum the lobes, I would be eternally grateful.

PHIL: We could go buy some.

EDDIE: I got plenty.

PHIL: She and me could go. I know where to buy it like it grows on trees.

BONNIE: I was in mortal longing for someone to call me. I was totally without hope of ever having worthwhile companionship tonight, a decent fucking conversation.
(PHIL *puts his arm around her as* EDDIE *spoons out some coke.*)

PHIL: Eddie's got some stuff here to really round off your— you know, rough spots.

BONNIE: I couldn't be happier.

PHIL: We been having a good time, too.

BONNIE: Is this particular guy just being ceremonial here with me, Eddie, or does he want to dick me?

EDDIE: I thought we'd get around to that later.

BONNIE (*to* PHIL): Eddie thought we'd get around to that later.

PHIL (*hands up in a sign of surrender, he is backing away until he is in the cage-like area above the couch, under the landing, the support beams like bars*): Hey, if I have overstepped some invisible boundary here, you notify me fast because I respond quickly to clear-cut information while, you know, murk and innuendo make me totally demented. (*To assuage his hurt feelings,* PHIL *does some coke.*)

ARTIE: We couldn't have less of any idea what we're doing here, Bonnie. (*As* MICKEY, *coming out of the bathroom, looks down on them.*)

BONNIE: I'm sure he has his saving graces.

MICKEY: Why don't you list them? I bet he'd like you to list them? (*With this,* MICKEY *breaks himself up;* ARTIE *erupts in giggles as if it's his joke and* PHIL, *whacked with the coke, joins in.*)

PHIL: You could make a list of what you think might be my saving graces based on some past savings account in the sky.

BONNIE: Is everybody ripped here?

MICKEY: We're involved in a wide variety of pharmaceutical experiments. (*This, of course, keeps them laughing, as he settles down into a languid sitting position against a banister strut, one foot dangling.*)

EDDIE: Testing the perimeters of the American Dream of oblivion.

BONNIE: Well, I can't express the gratitude for your generosity that led you to including me.

PHIL: You want people to call, you might spend less time on the phone.

BONNIE (*turning to look for* PHIL, *who is still lurking under the landing, she moves in his direction*): This is exactly my point. This bozo would not get off the phone.

PHIL: This explains the infinite length of your busy signal.

BONNIE: See! This is what I was afraid of. (*Passing behind the couch, she pets and straightens* ARTIE's *hair. This makes him very happy.*) Friends might call. You see the dilemma I was in.

PHIL (*almost scolding her*): Eddie called and called.

EDDIE (*from the counter where he's preparing a drink for* BONNIE): We called as if it was a religious duty.

BONNIE (*moving around to the front of the couch, she crosses back to* EDDIE *for her drink*): Thank God you persisted. This guy was pushing me beyond my own rational limits so I was into hallucinatory kinds of, you know, considerations. (*With her drink, she crosses to the armchair and sits.*) Like would I invite him over and then hack him to death with a cleaver.

PHIL: Who is this guy? (*Still under the landing.*) I know ways to make guys stop anything. They might think they couldn't live without it until I talk to them. They might think they have the courage of cowboys, but I can change their minds. Who is this guy?

BONNIE: This is what I'm getting at, Eddie, a person like this guy can only be found in your household. (*Clearly intrigued by* PHIL:) What was your name again?

PHIL: Phil. (*Encouraged, he is moving toward her now.*)

ARTIE: He's dangerous, Bonnie.

BONNIE: Who isn't?

ARTIE: I mean, in ways you can't imagine.

BONNIE: That's very unlikely, Artie.
(EDDIE, *settling onto the hassock, hands her a lighted joint.*)

Drugs. I mean, I'm telling this guy on the phone that drugs are and just have been as far as I can remember, an ever-present component of my personality. I am a drug person. And I would not, if I were him, consider that anything unusual, unless he is compelled to reveal to the entire world his ignorance of the current situation in which most people find themselves—so that's what I'm telling this guy.

PHIL: Who is this guy? (*As* PHIL *settles on the end of the coffee table, facing* BONNIE.) He's drivin' me nuts, this guy.

BONNIE: Some guy. Don't worry about it. (*Leaning to give* PHIL *a joint and to console him with her explanation.*) I mean, my life in certain of its segments has just moved into some form of automation on which it runs as if my input is no longer required. So my girlfriend Sarah gets involved with this guy who is totally freaked out on est, so she gets proportionally freaked out on est, this is what love can do to you. (*Getting the joint back from* PHIL, *she hands it to* EDDIE.) So then they are both attempting to freak me out on est, as if my certainty that they are utterly full of shit is some nonnegotiable threat to them rather than just my opinion and so they must—out of their insecurity—assault me with this goddamn EST ATTACK so that everywhere I turn I am confronted with their booklets and God knows what else, these pictures of this Werner Shmerner and the key to them that I must get rid of is my drug desires, which is the subject of their unending, unvaried, you know, whatchamacallit.

ARTIE, EDDIE, MICKEY: Proselytizing . . .
(*They say this overlapping.*)

BONNIE: They will not shut up about it. So finally I am trying to make to this guy what is for me an obvious point, which is that unlike those who have lost their minds to est, I am a normal person. I need my drugs. (*Rising, she moves to hand the joint up to* MICKEY *and wait for it to come back.*) And I am scoffed at for this remark, so, being civilized, I attempt to support my point with what Sarah and I both know from our mutual girlfriend Denise. "Does Denise not work as a legal secretary in this building full of lawyers?" I tell him. (*Moving to the back of the couch, she hands* ARTIE *the joint and waits for it.*) Well, she says these lawyers are totally blow oriented, and you go in there in the after-hours where some of them are still working, it sounds like a goddamn hog farm, she says. Well, Sarah and this guy react to this with two absolutely unaltered onslaughts, so while they're yelling at me, I'm yelling at them, that since I am a drug person, I must give them a drug person's answer: (*Having returned with the joint to* PHIL, *she hands it to him.*) "Thbgggggggggghhhhhhhhgggggghhhhh!" I go, and slam down the phone and hang it up. (*Laughing, she settles easily into his lap.*)

PHIL: So that's when we called.

BONNIE: When I picked it up, you were there. (*Glancing to* EDDIE.) Eddie was there.

PHIL: And now you're here.

MICKEY (*gazing down and gesturing toward* PHIL *and* BON-NIE): Is this the hand of destiny again, Eddie, look at it.

EDDIE (*on the hassock staring at them with delight*): I'm looking.

MICKEY: The hand of destiny again emerging just enough from, you know, all the normal muck and shit, so that, you know, we get a glimpse of it.

BONNIE: Whata you mean, Mickey? What's he mean?

EDDIE: It's a blind date.

BONNIE: Ohh, you invited me over for this guy, Eddie?

EDDIE: Yeah. Why?

BONNIE: Oh, you know, I thought . . .

PHIL: She don't have to, Eddie. (*Leaping to his feet,* PHIL *backs away, leaving* BONNIE *standing there.*)

BONNIE: No, no, I just didn't know it was a setup.

PHIL (*backing around the couch, he ends up under the landing*): I mean, she should know it could be the final straw for me to justify some sort of butchery, but that's just a fact of life and not in any way meant to influence the thing here.

EDDIE: You disappointed in Phil?

BONNIE: I wasn't thinking about it.

EDDIE: He's nervous.

PHIL (*up under the landing*): I'm very nervous.

BONNIE: Right. So what's the agenda?

EDDIE: Hey, I figured I'd just sort of rough in the outline, you'd
have the rest at your fingertips; you know, operating at
an instinctual level.

BONNIE (*turning to* PHIL): So you wanna go upstairs?
(PHIL *shakes his head no.*)

No?

PHIL: Out. Eddie, can I borrow your car? I don't have a car.

BONNIE: So we'll go over to my place. (*Picking up a joint from
the coffee table.*) Can I take this, Eddie?

EDDIE: What happened to your car?

PHIL: My wife got all the keys. She put one a those locks on it
so it fuckin' screams at you. (*He is putting on his coat
and sunglasses.*)

BONNIE: I got a car.

PHIL: You got a car?
(BONNIE *is hastening around, collecting supplies, picking up her shoes.*)

BONNIE: So we'll be back in a little, you guys'll be here?

EDDIE: Where else?

BONNIE: Bye.

MICKEY (*as* BONNIE *and* PHIL *go out the door*): Have a nice
time, kids.

EDDIE: Bye.

MICKEY: She's some bitch. (*Getting to his feet, heading into
his room.*)

EDDIE: Balloons. Balloons. (*Having walked toward the door,*
EDDIE, *with a bottle of bourbon and a glass, collapses
backward over the arm of the couch, so he ends up lying
with his head on a pillow almost on* ARTIE's *lap, his legs
dangling off the arm.*)

ARTIE (*lounging, his hands behind his head, he sits there,
staring off*): Eddie, can I ask you something? I wanna ask
you something.

EDDIE: Sure.

ARTIE: You don't mind?

EDDIE: What?

ARTIE: I'm just very curious about the nature of certain pat-
terns of bullshit by which people pull the wool over their
own eyes.

EDDIE: Yeah?

ARTIE: So could you give me a hint as to the precise nature of
the delusion with which you hype yourself about this
guy, that you treat him the way you do?

EDDIE: Artie, hey, you know, I have a kind of intuitive thing with Phil. Don't get in a fuckin' snit about it.

ARTIE: Because you desert me for this fucking guy all the time. What is it about you, you gotta desert me?

EDDIE: I don't desert you.

ARTIE: But what is it you really think about me, so that in your estimation you can dump on me, and treat Phil like he's some—I don't know what—but you lost a paternity suit and he was the result.

EDDIE: Artie, first of all, I don't consider your statement that I dump on you accurate, so why should I defend against it?

ARTIE: It's subtle. Hey, you think that means I'm gonna miss it? It's an ongoing, totally pervasive attitude with which you dump on me subtly so that it colors almost every remark, every gesture. And I'm sick of it.

EDDIE (*reaching up, he pats* ARTIE'S *arm*): I'm sorry your deal fell through.

ARTIE: You lie to yourself, Eddie.

EDDIE: Yeah?

ARTIE: That's right. You lie to yourself.

EDDIE: Just because you're Jewish doesn't make you Freud, you prick.

ARTIE: And just because you're whatever the fuck you are doesn't make you whatever the hell you think you are. The goddamn embodiment of apple pie here is full of shit.

EDDIE: So I lie, huh? Who better? I'm a very good liar, and I'm very gullible.

ARTIE: And my deal didn't fall through, anyway. That's just stunningly diversionary on your part even if it did. Which it didn't. (*As* MICKEY, *wandering out of his room, leans on the railing to look down on them.*) You're a deceptive sonofabitch, Eddie. Is everything a ploy to you?

EDDIE: What are you talking about?

ARTIE: You know what I mean.

EDDIE: I don't.

ARTIE: The hell you don't. Doesn't he, Mickey? He knows.

EDDIE: I don't. I swear it.

ARTIE (*leaping to his feet*): You're just avoiding the goddamn confrontation here.

EDDIE: What confrontation?

ARTIE: We're having a confrontation here.

EDDIE: We are?

ARTIE: Yeah! I am! I'm gettin' out of here. Mickey, you wanna get out of here?

MICKEY: Sure. (MICKEY *heads off into his room as* ARTIE *lunges up the stairs.*)

EDDIE: Where you goin'?

ARTIE: I'm goin' to the can, and then I'm getting out of here. (*Halfway up the stairs, he whirls to face* EDDIE:) And you, you sonofabitch, I'm going to tell you the goddamn bottom line because if you don't know it, you are—I mean, a thousandfold—just utterly—and you fucking know it!

EDDIE: You're a schmuck, Artie.

ARTIE: (*on the balcony, looking down on* EDDIE): Hey, you don't have to deal any further with my attempts at breathing life into this corpse of our friendship. Forget about it. (*He bolts into the bathroom as* MICKEY, *tucking in a nice clean shirt, comes out of his room.*)

EDDIE: You're a schmuck, Artie! You're a schmendrick! (*The bathroom door slams.*)

Go check your messages! (*Lying on the couch from which he has not budged.*) What was that?

MICKEY (*leaning on the railing, looking down*): I think what he was trying to get at is that he, you know, considers your investment in Phil, which is in his mind sort of disproportionate and maybe even—and mind you, this is Artie's thought, not mine—but maybe even fraudulent and secretly self-serving on your part. So you know, blah-blah-blah, rapateta—that this investment is based on the fact that Phil is very safe because no matter how far you manage to fall, Phil will be lower. You end up crawling along the sidewalk, Phil's gonna be on his belly in the gutter looking up in wide-eyed admiration. (*As* MICKEY, *carrying his glass, is now heading down the stairs.*)

EDDIE: This is what Artie thinks?

MICKEY (*he settles on the couch into the exact spot that* ARTIE

vacated, picking up a bottle from the coffee table and
pouring himself a drink, emptying the bottle): Yeah.
And it hurts his feelings, because, you know, he'd like to
think he might be capable of an eyeball-to-eyeball relationship with you based not necessarily on equality, but
on, nevertheless, some real affinity—and if not the actu-
ality, at least the possibility of respect. So your, you
know, decision, or whatever—compulsion—to short-
change yourself in his estimation and hang out with Phil
is for him a genuine disappointment, which you just saw
the manifestation of.

EDDIE: That was his hurt feelings.

MICKEY: Yeah.

EDDIE: What's everybody on my case for all of a sudden?

MICKEY: Nobody's on your case.

EDDIE (*sitting up to look at* MICKEY): What do you think
   you're doing, then, huh? What is this? What was Artie
   doing?

MICKEY: You have maybe some misconceptions is all, first of
   all about how smart you are. And then maybe even if you
   are as smart as you think you are, you have some mis-
   conception about what that entitles you to regarding
   your behavior to other human beings. Such facts being
   pointed out is what's going on here, that's all. Don't take
   it personally.

EDDIE: What would make you mad, Mickey? (*Leaning, he*
   pokes at MICKEY's *hair.*)

MICKEY: Hey, I'm sure it's possible.

EDDIE: What would it be? I'm trying to imagine.

MICKEY: The truth is, Artie isn't really that pissed at you anyway.

EDDIE: He got close enough. (*Getting to his feet.*)

MICKEY: You know, his feelings got hurt.

EDDIE: That's what I'm talking about. (*Crossing to the kitchen counter to open a new bottle.*) Don't I have feelings, too?

MICKEY (*trailing along to get some ice for his drink*): Except that it makes him feel good to have his feelings hurt, that's why he likes you. You're a practicing prick. You berate him with this concoction of moral superiority which no doubt reassures him everything is as it should be, sort of reminding him in a cozy way of his family in whose eyes he basked most of his life as a glowing disappointment. (*MICKEY is now seated on a stool on the downstage side of the nook while EDDIE leans on the stage right edge of the L.*)

EDDIE: You're just too laid back for human tolerance sometimes, Mickey. A person wonders if you really care.

MICKEY: I get excited. (*Pouring a little coke onto the side of his hand which he snorts.*)

EDDIE: You have it figured somehow. What's it according to— some schematic arrangement—grids of sophistication— what's the arrangement by which you assess what's what so you are left utterly off the hook?

MICKEY: It's a totally unconscious process. (*Pouring a little more coke onto the side of his hand.*)

EDDIE: Fuck you, Mickey.

MICKEY: Ask Darlene if she won't let you go back to coke, why don't you? Booze seems to bring out some foul-spirited streak in you. (*Putting the coke on his hand in front of* EDDIE's *nose.*)

EDDIE (*knocking the coke aside*): Don't you talk about her, okay! Don't you fucking talk to me about Darlene! (*He moves toward the stairs and starts to climb them.*) That's the fucking bottom line, though, huh, nobody's going to take substantial losses in order to align and endure with what are totally peripheral—I mean, transient—elements in their life. We all know we don't mean shit in one another's eyes, finally. (*On the landing, he tosses the last little bit of his drink at* MICKEY, *sitting by the counter.*)

MICKEY (*calmly picking up a towel to wipe his shirt*): You gonna remember any of this tomorrow, or is this one of your, you know, biodegradable moments?

EDDIE: Lemme in on your point of view, Mickey, we can have a dialectic.

MICKEY (*climbing the stairs past* EDDIE, *he hangs the towel on* EDDIE's *shoulder*): Hey. Just in case you notice me walk out of the room, you can reflect back on this, all right?

EDDIE: All right. On what? (*Tossing the towel into the kitchen.*)

MICKEY: That, you know, this foul mood of yours might have been sufficient provocation to motivate my departure, see. You know, lock that in so you can minimize the paranoia. (*Unbuttoning his shirt, he goes into his room.*)

EDDIE: You sound like my goddamn mother.

ARTIE (*as coming out of the bathroom, he heads down the stairs*): Father.

EDDIE (*starting up the rest of the stairs*): Mother.

ARTIE: So you coming with us, Eddie, or not? (*Passing* EDDIE *on the stairs.*)

EDDIE (*stopping to look down at* ARTIE): Where you going?

ARTIE: I don't know. (*As* MICKEY, *pulling a clean T-shirt on, comes out the door of his room.*) Where we going, Mickey?

MICKEY: It was your idea.

EDDIE: No.

MICKEY (*passing* EDDIE *on the stairs*): We'll go somewhere. We'll think of somewhere; change the mood.

EDDIE (*stomping down the stairs toward the couch and TV*): No. Fuck no. I'm gonna get ripped and rant at the tube.

MICKEY: What's a matter with you?

EDDIE: Nothing.

ARTIE: You don't wanna.

EDDIE: No. (*As* MICKEY *goes out the door.*)

ARTIE: You gonna be all right?

EDDIE (*turning on the TV, he flops down on the couch*): Who cares?

ARTIE: This is not caring I'm expressing here. (*Heading over to the kitchen counter.*) This is curiosity. Don't misconstrue the behavior here and confuse yourself that anybody cares!

MICKEY (*he steps back in the door*): Artie, let's go.

EDDIE (*as* ARTIE *does a line of coke on the counter*): Artie, relax. You're starting to sound like an imitation of yourself, and you're hardly tolerable the first time.

ARTIE (*doing a second line of coke on his hand, as* MICKEY *stands by the door watching the TV*): Eddie, don't worry about a thing. This is just some sort of irreversible chemical pollution of your soul. Your body has just gone into shock from all the shit you've taken in. (*As the phone starts to ring.*) So you're suffering some form of virulent terminal toxic nastiness. Nothing to worry about.
(ARTIE, *with his last word, is out the door. The phone is ringing.* EDDIE *is already on his way toward it.*)

EDDIE: Who's worried? The only thing worrying me, Artie, was that you might decide to stay. (*Grabbing up the phone.*) Yeah. Agnes. Whata you want? (*As he talks, he makes his way to the armchair carrying a bottle, staring at the TV, settling into the armchair.*) I said, were you worried I might be having a pleasant evening, you didn't want to take any chances that I might not be miserable enough without hearing from you? No, I did not make an obscene call to you. What'd he say? It can't be too dirty to say, Agnes, HE said it. Every call you make to me is obscene. (*With the remote, he turns off the TV.*) Everything you say to me is obscene. Of course I'm drunk. If you don't want to talk to me when I'm drunk, call me in the daytime. I'm sober in the daytime, but of course we both know you do want to talk to me when I'm drunk. You get off on it, don't you. Reminds you of the good old days. If you hurt my little girl, I'll kill you . . .

BONNIE (*from off*): Eddie . . . !

EDDIE (*into the phone*): I said, "If you hurt my little girl, I'll kill you!"
(BONNIE *enters through the front door, her clothing ripped and dirty, her knee scraped. Limping, she carries one of her shoes along with the scarf she wore.*)

BONNIE: Eddie . . . !

EDDIE (*into the phone*): I have to go. I'll call you tomorrow. Goodbye.
(*He hurries toward* BONNIE, *who, leaning against one of the balcony support beams, starts hobbling toward him, dragging the scarf that was in her hair when she arrived.*)

Where's Phil?

BONNIE: You know, Eddie, how come you gotta put me at the mercy of such a creep for? Can I ask you that?

EDDIE: Where is he? (*He runs to look out the door.*)

BONNIE: He threw me out of my own car, Eddie.

EDDIE (*whirling, he heads back to her*): What'd you do?

BONNIE (*settling into the armchair*): Whata you mean, what'd I do? He's a fucking guy, he should be in a ward somewhere! You could have at least warned me!

EDDIE: Nobody listens to me. (*Kneeling, he looks at her knee.*)

BONNIE: I listen to you and you damn well know it.

EDDIE: You're all right. (*Patting her, he heads for the bar to make her a drink and dampen a washcloth.*)

BONNIE: I'm alive, if that's what you mean, but I am haunted by the suspicion that it is strictly a matter of luck. I mean, you should reconsider your entire evaluation of this guy, Eddie. This is a guy, he is totally without redeeming social value!

EDDIE: Where is he?

BONNIE: He's a debilitating experience, this guy. I mean, I came down here in good faith, Eddie, I hope you are not going to miss that point.

EDDIE (*handing her the drink, he kneels down to tend her knee with the washcloth*): Will you get off your high horse about Phil, all right? So he took your car, so what. He'll bring it back.

BONNIE: He didn't just take my car, Eddie; HE THREW ME OUT OF IT.

EDDIE (*trying to shrug the whole thing off*): So what?

BONNIE (*ripping the washcloth from his hands*): Whata you mean, "So what?"

EDDIE: So what? (*Reaching to get the washcloth back.*)

BONNIE: Eddie, it was moving!

EDDIE: He slowed it down, I bet. (*Still he tries to get the washcloth, but she will not let him have it.*)

BONNIE: Right. He slowed it down. But he didn't slow it down enough. I mean, he didn't stop the fucking car. He slowed it down. Whata you mean "he slowed it down"? As if that was enough to make a person feel, you know, appropriately handled. He threw me out of my own slowly moving car and nearly killed me.

EDDIE (*indicating her knee, which is right in front of him*): You scraped your knee!

BONNIE: I just missed cracking open my head on a boulder that was beside the road.

EDDIE: What boulder?

BONNIE: Whata you mean, what boulder? This boulder beside the road. THAT boulder.

EDDIE: Will you please get to the fucking point? (*Once more after the towel.*)

BONNIE (*hitting him with the washcloth*): No.

EDDIE: Then shut up! (*He flops drunkenly backward.*)

BONNIE: No! (*Rising now, she starts to angrily pull off her skirt and then her pantyhose in order to tend to her knee and other scrapes.*) Because what I wanna know about maybe is you, and why you would put a friend of yours like me in that kind of jeopardy. Why you would let me go with this creep, if I was begging, let alone instigate it, that's what I'm wondering when I get right down to it, though I hadn't even thought about it. But maybe it's having a goddamn friendship with you is the source of jeopardy for a person!? (*Swinging her skirt at him, she storms over to the bar for more to drink, for water and ice for her aches and pains.*)

EDDIE: You want to take that position, go ahead.

BONNIE: I'm not sayin' I want to. I'm saying maybe I should want to, and if I think about it, maybe that's what I'll do and you ought to know I am going to think about it. I hurt my foot, too, and my hip and my elbow along with my knee.
(*Due to his drinking, EDDIE has been reacting increasingly as a little boy. Scolded by ARTIE and scolded by MICKEY, he tries to hold his ground against BONNIE, yet he wants to placate her. When she yells at him, he winces, as if her words are physical. Behind her back he sometimes mimics her as she talks. When she, out of her own frustration, swings at him with a shoe, a blouse, her pantyhose, he recoils as a child might.*)

EDDIE: I'm sorry about that.

BONNIE: Maybe you might show something more along the lines of your feelings and how you might explain yourself. (*Coming around to the front of the bar, she sits on a stool.*) I mean, this guy, Eddie, is not just, you know, semi-weird; he is working on genuine berserk. Haven't you noticed some clue to this?

EDDIE: You must have done SOMETHING. (*Crawling to the couch.*)

BONNIE: I SAT THERE. (*She puts her foot up on another stool and tends her knee.*) He drove; I listened to the music on the tape deck like he wanted, and I tol' him the sky was pretty, just trying, you know, to put some sort of fucking humanity into the night, some sort of spirit so we might,

you know, appear to one another as having had at one
time or another a thought in our heads and were not just
these totally fuck-oriented, you know, things with
clothes on.

EDDIE: What are you getting at?

BONNIE: What I'm getting at is I did nothing, and in addition, I
am normally a person who allots a certain degree of my
energy to being on the alert for creeps, Eddie. I am not so
dumb as to be ignorant of the vast hordes of creeps
running loose in California as if every creep with half
his screws loose has slid here like the continent is tilted.
(*Crossing to* EDDIE, *who is sitting on the couch.*) But
because this guy was on your recommendation, I am
caught unawares and nearly maimed. That's what I'm
getting at. I mean, this guy is driving, so I tell him we
can go to my house. He says he's hungry, so I say, "Great,
how about a Jack-in-the-Box?" He asks me if that's a code
for something. So I tell him, "No, it's California-talk, we
have a million of 'em, is he new in town?" His answer is,
do I have a water bed? "No," I tell him, but we could go to
a sex motel, they got water beds. They got porn on the in-
house video. Be great! So then I detect he's lookin' at me,
so I smile, and he says, "Whata you smilin' about?" I say,
"Whata you mean?" He says, like he's talkin' to the
steering wheel, "Whata you thinkin'?" or some shit. I
mean, but it's like to the steering wheel; he's all bent out
of shape.

EDDIE: See. (*Staring at her, he rises.*) You did something.

BONNIE: What?

EDDIE: I don't know.

BONNIE: I smiled.

EDDIE: Then what?

BONNIE (*as he paces behind her, watching her, saying, "Yeah, yeah" every now and then*): I smiled, Eddie, for chrissake, I smiled is what I did. It's a friendly thing in most instances, but for him it promotes all this paranoid shit he claims he can read in it my secret opinions of him, which he is now saying. (*As* EDDIE *moves away toward the bar, she follows.*) The worst things anybody could think about anybody, but I ain't saying nothing. He's sayin' it. Then he screams he knew this venture was a one-man operation and the next thing I know he's trying to push me out of the car. He's trying to drive it, and slow it down, and push me out all at once, so we're swervin' all over the road.
(*At the bar, they have ended with* EDDIE *on the inside of the L and* BONNIE *outside, on the stage right side as he is getting himself a drink.*)

So that's what happened. You get it now?

EDDIE: He's been having a rough time.

BONNIE: Eddie, it's a rough century all the way around—you say so yourself, Eddie. Who does anybody know who is doing okay? So this is some sort of justification for us all to start pushing each other out of cars?—things aren't working out personally the way we planned?

EDDIE (*banging the bottle on the bar, he comes around to the front*): Aren't you paying any fucking attention to my point here? I'm talking about a form of desperation you are maybe not familiar with it.

BONNIE: Oh.

EDDIE (*pacing down to the armchair into which he flops*): I'm talking about a man here, a guy he's had his entire thing collapse. Phil has been driven to the brink.

BONNIE: Oh. Okay. *(She storms to the couch where her clothes lie on the floor and she begins to dress.)* You consider desperation you and your friend's own, private, so-called thingamajig. Who would have thought other? I mean, I can even understand that due to the attitude I know you hold me in, which is of course mainly down. Because deep down, a person does not live in an aura of— you know, which we all have them, auras—and they spray right out of us and they are just as depressing and pushy on the people in our company as anything we might, you know, knowingly and overtly bad-mouth them with. But at the same time, you certainly should be told that in my opinion you are totally, one hundred percent, you know, with your head up your ass about me.

EDDIE: Yeah.

BONNIE: That's what I'm saying. "Wrong," is what I'm saying. See, because I am a form of human being just like any other, get it! And you wanna try holding on to things on the basis of your fingernails, give me a call. So desperation, believe it or not, is within my areas of expertise, you understand? I am a person whose entire life with a child to support depends on her tits and this balloon and the capabilities of her physical grace and imaginary inventiveness with which I can appear to express something of interest in the air by my movement and places in the air I put the balloon along with my body, which some other dumb bitch would be unable to imagine or would fall down in the process of attempting to perform in front of crowds of totally incomprehensible and terrifying bunch of audience members. And without my work what am I but an unemployed scrunt on the meat market of the streets? Because this town is nothin' but mean in spite of the palm trees. (*Rooting in the armchair for the scarf she carried in and left in the armchair where she first sat, she forces* EDDIE *to leave the chair.*) So that's my point about desperation, and I can give you references, just in case you never thought of it, you know; and just thought I was over here—some mindless twat over here with blonde hair and big eyes.

EDDIE (*having picked the* TV Guide *off the coffee table, he turns on the TV and flops down on the couch*): I hadn't noticed your hair or eyes.

BONNIE: I'm gonna level with you, Eddie, I came here for a ride home and an apology. (*Finished dressing, she starts for the door.*)

EDDIE: Don't you fuck everybody you meet?

BONNIE: Whata you mean? WHAT?

EDDIE: You know what I'm talking about.

BONNIE (*coming toward the back of the couch*): I fuck who I want. What does one thing have to do with—I mean, what's the correlation, huh?

EDDIE: You fuck everybody.

BONNIE: I fuck a lot of different guys: that's just what I do. It's interesting. You learn a lot about 'em. That's no reason to assume I can be thrown out of a car as random recreation, however. If I want to jump, I'll jump. Not that that's the point, I hope.

EDDIE: It's not far from it.

BONNIE (*joining him on the couch to make her point*): I

mean, I fuck different guys so I know the difference. That's what I'm saying. There's a lot of little subtleties go right by you don't have nothing to compare them to.

EDDIE: But you're getting these airs is what I'm getting at. I mean you're assuming some sort of posture, like some attitude of I pushed you into some terrible, unfamiliar circumstances and normally you're very discreet about who you ball and who you don't, when normally you—

BONNIE: He coulda hurt me, Eddie.

EDDIE: I don't care!

BONNIE: Don't tell me that.

EDDIE: You're just some bitch who thinks it matters that you run around with balloons and your tits out.
(*Rising,* BONNIE *crosses to the counter, to snort some coke.*)

Nobody's going to take substantial losses over what are totally peripheral, totally transient elements. You know, we're all just background in one another's life. Cardboard cutouts bumping around in this vague, you know, hurlyburly, this spin-off of what was once prime-time life; so don't hassle me about this interpersonal fuck-up on the highway, okay?

BONNIE: You oughta have some pity. (*Crossing toward the door to leave.*)

EDDIE: I'm savin' it.

BONNIE: For your buddies.

EDDIE: For myself.

(BONNIE *steps out and then right back in running, hobbling.* PHIL *bursts in wearing his sport coat and sunglasses.*)

BONNIE: Oh, no. (BONNIE *flees, ending up near the phone, as* EDDIE *rises from the couch, turning off the TV and trying to move to* PHIL.)

PHIL: I'm perfectly, you know, back to earth now. I can understand if you don't believe me, but there's nothing to be concerned about.

BONNIE: I oughta call the cops, you prick.

PHIL: Your car's just outside; it's okay. (*He is very excited, very much a take-charge guy.*)

BONNIE: I'm talking about murder almost.

PHIL (*running to grab the phone and give it to her, as she flees to the inside of the nook*): You want me to dial it for you, Bonnie; you have every right.

EDDIE: Shut up. Can you do that? CAN YOU JUST SHUT UP? (*Unable to catch up with* PHIL, *he stands center stage, yelling at the both of them.*)

PHIL: I'm sorry, Eddie.

EDDIE: I mean, I'm disgusted with the both of you.

PHIL: I don't blame you, Eddie.

EDDIE: I did my best for the both of you. I did everything I could to set you up nicely, but you gotta fuck it up. Why is that?

PHIL: I'm some kind of very, very unusual jerk, is what I figure.

BONNIE: You had no rhyme nor reason for what you did to me.

PHIL (*he will explain it, he will take charge, crossing as if he is about to go to the door*): It's broads, Eddie. I got all this hubbub for a personality with which I try to make do, but they see right through it to where I am invisible. I see 'em see through; it makes me crazy, but it ain't their fault.

EDDIE: I go out of my way for you, Phil; I don't know what more I can do. Now I have Artie pissed at me, I have Bonnie pissed.

PHIL: She has every right; you have every right. Artie's pissed, too?

EDDIE: You know that.

PHIL: I didn't know it.

EDDIE: In your heart I'm talkin' about, Phil; that's what I'm talking about.

PHIL (*swaggering to the armchair, he sits*): It's—you know, my imaginary side, Eddie—like we were sayin', I get lost in it. (*Bragging, he takes off his glasses, crosses his legs, sticking the glasses into the jacket pocket.*) I gotta channel it into my work more.

EDDIE (*standing there*): Fuck your work. What work? You don't have any work, Phil, you're background, don't you know that? They just take you on for background. They got all these bullshit stories they want to fill the air with, they want to give them some sense of reality, some fucking air of authenticity, don't they? So they take some guy like you and stick him around the set to make the whole load of shit look real. Don't you know that? You're a prop. (*Moving to the counter, he grabs a vial of coke and starts putting a line on his hand.*) The more guys like you they got looking like the truth, the more bullshit they can spread all around you. You're like a tree, Phil. You're like the location! They just use you to make the bullshit look legitimate!

PHIL: What about my, you know, talent; you said I ought to . . . you know . . . Remember?

EDDIE (*he snorts some coke*): That was hype. I don't know what I was doin'.

PHIL: Oh.

EDDIE: Hype. You know.

PHIL: You were what—puttin' me on?

EDDIE (*moving to the couch with the coke*): This is the real goods.

PHIL: You mean, all that you said about how I oughta, you know, have some faith in myself, it wasn't true.

EDDIE: Whata you think? Did you ever really believe it?

PHIL: Yeah. Sorta.

EDDIE: Not really. No. (*He does some coke.*)

PHIL: Well, you know. No.

EDDIE: So who we been kiddin'?

PHIL: Me. We been kiddin' me. But this is the real goods . . . now, right? I mean we're gettin' down to the real goods now.

EDDIE: Yeah.

PHIL (*very assertive, very confident*): So you musta decided it would be best for me to hear the truth.

EDDIE: Naw.

PHIL: So I could try and straighten myself out.

EDDIE: I'm just sick of you, Phil.

PHIL: Oh. How long you been sick of me? (*Very assertive, very confident.*) It's probably recent.

EDDIE: No.

PHIL: So it's been a long time . . . So what caused it?

EDDIE: I'm gonna let you off the hook now, Phil. I'm not gonna say any more. (*Doing some more coke.*)

PHIL (*standing*): You gotta.

EDDIE: I'm gonna lighten up. (*He picks up a newspaper from off the coffee table as if he will read.*) I'm gonna give you a break.

PHIL (*crossing to* EDDIE, *he picks up the empty bourbon bottle from the coffee table*): Eddie, you gotta give me the entire thing now. I don't need a break. (*He pushes* EDDIE.) I want it all. I can take it. (*He pokes* EDDIE *in the back of the head.*) It's for my own good, right? (*He rips the paper from* EDDIE'S *hand, he slaps* EDDIE *in the back of the head.*) I can take it. I gotta have it. I got a tendency to kid myself everything is okay. (*He hits him, all the while holding the bottle by the neck as a club.*) So, you know, you tell me what are the things about me that are for you, you know, disgusting. I want to know. (*He hits again, again.*) Tell me what they are.

EDDIE (*looking up at* PHIL): Everything. Everything about you.

PHIL: Everything? Everything? (*He starts to laugh, he falls down onto the couch, laughing, clutching* EDDIE.) You really had me fooled, Eddie.

EDDIE: That was the point.

BONNIE (*from behind the kitchen counter where she has watched this whole thing*): You guys are crazy.

EDDIE: Whata you mean? (*Looking drunkenly at* PHIL, *who is hugging him.*) What does she mean? You . . . look terrible, Phil.

BONNIE: You ain't lookin' so good yourself, Eddie.

EDDIE: I feel awful.

BONNIE: Whatsamatter?

EDDIE: I dunno. I'm depressed.

PHIL: What about?

EDDIE: Everything. (*Picking the newspaper up off the table.*) You read this shit?! Look at this shit!

PHIL: You depressed about the news, Eddie?

EDDIE: Yeah.

PHIL: You depressed about the newspaper, Eddie?

EDDIE: It's depressing. You read about this fucking neutron bomb? Look at this. (*Hands a part of the paper to* PHIL, *pointing to an article.*)

PHIL: It's depressing.

EDDIE: Yeah. (*He snorts some coke.*)

BONNIE: It's depressing. The newspaper is very depressing. I get depressed every time I read it.
(*There is an element of hope in both* BONNIE *and* PHIL *that* EDDIE *may explain things.*)

EDDIE (*blasted with the coke now, these ideas burst from him*): I mean, not that I would suggest that, you know, the anxiety of this age is an unprecedented anxiety, but I'm fucking worried about it, you know. (*Spreading coke on his hand and offering it to* BONNIE *as she is edging closer.*)

PHIL: So it's the neutron bomb got you down, huh, Eddie?

EDDIE:
(PHIL *is reading the paper as* BONNIE *snorts some coke off* EDDIE*'s hand.* EDDIE *then meticulously rips an article from the paper* PHIL *holds; he hands the article to* BON-NIE *to read.*)

I mean, the aborigine had a lot of problems—nobody is going to say he didn't—tigers in the trees, dogs after his food; and in the Middle Ages, there was goblins and witches in the woods. But this neutron bomb has come along and this sonofabitch has got this ATTITUDE. (*He does some coke and blasts on.*) I mean, inherent in the conception of it is this fucking ATTITUDE about what is worthwhile in the world and what is worth preserving. And do you know what this fastidious prick has at the top of its hierarchy—what sits at the pinnacle? THINGS! Put one down in the vicinity of this room and we're out. The three of us—out, out, out! (*Suddenly nauseous, he bolts for the waste can beside the stage left leg of the counter, and he kneels there but doesn't vomit, then leaps to his feet.*) But guess what? The glasses don't even crack. The telephone's fine. The chairs, the table— (*He moves along the counter, racing with the effect of the coke, carrying the waste can, banging the counter, the stools, the "things."*) The things are un-fucking-disturbed. It annihilates people and saves THINGS. It loves things. It is a thing that loves things. And whether we know it or not, we KNOW it—that's eating at us. (*He is heading up the stairs to the bathroom.*) And where other, older, earlier people—(*now he dashes back down to the record player for his dictionary, then heads back up the stairs*)—the Ancients might have had some consolation from a view of the heavens as inhabited by this thoughtful, you know, meditative, maybe a trifle unpredictable and wrathful, but nevertheless UP THERE—this divine onlooker—we have bureaucrats who are devoted to the accumulation of incomprehensible data—we have connoisseurs of graft and the three-martini lunch for whom we vote on the basis of their media consultants. The air's bad, the ozone's fucked, the water's poison, and into whose eyes do we find ourselves staring when we look for providence? (*Leaving the waste can on the stairs near the top, he bolts through the banister.*) We have emptied out the heavens and put oblivion in the hands of a bunch of aging insurance salesmen whose jobs are insecure. (*Disappearing into the bathroom.*)

BONNIE: Yeah, well, Eddie, it's no reason to be mean to your friends.

EDDIE (*from off*): Says you.

BONNIE: Exactly.

PHIL (*somewhere during* EDDIE's *speech,* PHIL *has dozed off and now he jumps to his feet, startling* BONNIE, *who, seated on the couch next to* PHIL, *leaps to her feet, watching his every unpredictable move*): I gotta get something from the car. (*He runs for the door.*)

EDDIE (*from off*): WHAT?

PHIL: I'll be right back. (*As* EDDIE *comes staggering out the bathroom door, trying to read his dictionary.*)

BONNIE: Boy, Eddie, you are just transforming right before my eyes, and I used to have an entirely optimistic opinion of you. I mean, I feel like a goddamn magnifying glass couldn't find what's left of your good points. (*She is climbing the stairs toward him.*) What is going on with you?

EDDIE: Suck my dick.

BONNIE: I'm being serious here, Eddie, I thought you had this girlfriend and it was a significant, you know, mutually fulfilling relationship, but you're hardly a viable social entity at the moment, that's what I think.

EDDIE (*he tosses the dictionary to the floor; tugging at the zipper of his fly, he moves toward her*): Things have taken a turn for the worse, that's all. Suck my dick, Bonnie. (*He reaches for her head, she pushes him in the chest and down he goes to the floor, a wreck.*)

BONNIE: Like what?

EDDIE: Who'm I going to complain to? (*Crawling to the front edge of the banister, looking for his waste can.*) Who's listenin'? And even if they are, what can they do about it? (*As he gropes for the waste can on the stairs, she hands it to him.*)

BONNIE: I'm listenin'.

EDDIE: She doesn't love me. (*He lies there, his head over the edge, the waste can dangling from his hand.*)

BONNIE: Who?

EDDIE: My girlfriend.

BONNIE: Whata you mean?

EDDIE: Whata you mean, whata I mean? She doesn't love me. Is that some sort of arcane, totally off-the-wall, other-worldly sentiment that I am some oddity to find distressing so that nobody to whom I mention it has any personal reference by which they can understand me? What is going on here? My girlfriend doesn't love me.

BONNIE: Sure she does.

EDDIE: No.

BONNIE: Why?

EDDIE: I don't know, but she doesn't.

BONNIE: Are you sure?

EDDIE (*dropping the waste can, he struggles to sit up*): She's out of town all the time. She's always out of town. She takes every job that comes across her desk, you know, as long as it takes her out of town.

BONNIE: So you miss her.

EDDIE: She's a photographer, you know. Fuck her. There's pictures here. It's Hollywood.

BONNIE: Sure. You should tell her.

EDDIE (*sitting there, his legs dangling over the edge of the balcony, he is framed in the square of the railing*): Talking about love makes you feel like you're watching TV, Bonnie . . . (*noticing the railing framing him, he realizes he looks like a TV image*) that why you're so interested? I'm real, Bonnie. I'm not a goddamn TV image in front of you, here. (*He starts to pound his legs, having a little fit.*) This is real. I'm a real person, Bonnie, you know that, right? Suck my dick.

BONNIE (*he is reaching for her; she pushes him away and heads down the stairs*): You know, if your manner of speech is in any way a reflection of what goes on in your head, Eddie, it's a wonder you can tie your shoes.

EDDIE (*following her*): You're right. You ever have that experience where your thoughts are like these totally separate, totally self-sustaining phone booths in this vast uninhabited shopping mall in your head? You ever have that experience? (*He half crawls, half falls over the back of the couch, ending up lying there.*) My inner monologue has taken on certain disquieting characteristics, I mean, I don't feel loved. Even if she loves me, I don't feel it. I don't feel loved, and I'm sick of it, you know what I mean?

BONNIE: I'm gonna go.

EDDIE: What for?

BONNIE: Home. I'm going home. (*She starts to remove his shoes.*) Maybe you been doin' too much shit, Eddie. Even outlaws have to take precautionary measures.

EDDIE (*he pulls away*): No. I say, "no." You want me "Good." "Kinder." "More considerate." But I say no. I will be a thing and live. Be harder, colder, a rock or polyurethane, that's my advice. Be a thing and live . . . that's my advice . . .
(ARTIE *and* MICKEY *come in the door.* MICKEY, *drinking a soda through a straw, heads up to his room, while* ARTIE, *carrying two large Burger King bags, goes to the kitchen for a cup of coffee.*)

MICKEY: Hi.

ARTIE: Hey.

BONNIE: I'm going home.

MICKEY: How was your date?

ARTIE (*mocking her as he passes her*): We saw your date out in the bushes there like a madman. What's the haps, here, huh?

BONNIE: The hell with the bunch of you. (*She heads for the door.*)

EDDIE (*still lying on the couch*): He threw her out of her car. (*This startles* ARTIE *as he realizes the date did not go well: good news for him.*)

BONNIE (*rushing back to scold* EDDIE): Can't you just keep your mouth shut, Eddie? Does everybody have to know?

EDDIE: Suck my dick.

BONNIE: Goodbye.

ARTIE (*a Burger King bag still in his hands*): Whata you doin' tomorrow, Bonnie?

BONNIE: Why?

ARTIE: I wanna know.

BONNIE: I don't wanna tell you, it's none of your business, I'm taking my kid to Disneyland. We're goin' for the day, so I won't be home.

EDDIE: You haven't been to Disneyland yet?

BONNIE: Of course we been. We been a hundred times. We like it.

ARTIE: I'll go with you?

BONNIE: You wanna?

ARTIE: Sure.

BONNIE: Great. Come by about eleven.

ARTIE: Okay.

BONNIE: Bye.
 (*As she goes out the door,* MICKEY *comes down the stairs and crosses into the kitchen to join* ARTIE *at the Burger King bags.*)

MICKEY: Bye.

ARTIE: Bye.

EDDIE: You guys see Phil outside?

ARTIE (*to* MICKEY): So she likes to be thrown out of cars. I threw a bitch out of bed once.

EDDIE: It ain't the same thing.

ARTIE: Did I say it was?

MICKEY: What happened?

EDDIE: You implied it.

ARTIE: She was harassing me. We were ballin' away, she's
tellin' me, "Faster, faster, slower, higher, do this, do that.
Faster. Higher." So I says to her, "Hey, listen, am I in your
way here, or what?"
(*The front door opens, and* PHIL *comes in carrying a
baby wrapped in a blanket.*)

PHIL: I got my baby.

ARTIE: What?

PHIL: I got my baby.

MICKEY: Phil.

ARTIE: He got this kid. You got your kid, Phil.

MICKEY: Where's your wife?

PHIL: Sleepin'. (*He has rushed like a thief, moving with speed
and stealth straight to the armchair, where he sits cradling the baby.*)

MICKEY: She doesn't know? (*Tentatively,* ARTIE *and* MICKEY
move to gather around PHIL *and peek at the baby.*)

PHIL: I snuck. I coulda been anybody. I coulda done anything.
You like her?

ARTIE: You kidnapped her.

PHIL (*half rising, his voice low in order not to wake the baby*):

You want me to kill you, Artie? This is my baby here. She's mine.

MICKEY (*placating* PHIL, *distracting him from the anger*): She looks like you, Phil.

ARTIE: Around the eyes.

MICKEY: And the mouth. Look at the mouth. That's Phil's mouth.

PHIL: I don't see it.

ARTIE: It's unmistakable.

MICKEY: You don't see it in the eyes?

PHIL: No, I look real hard, and I try like to think I'm looking into my own eyes, but I don't see anything of my own at all. I wish I did. Nothing familiar. Just this baby. Cute. But like I found her.

ARTIE: Look how she's looking at you.

PHIL: They can't see. It's the sound vibrations and this big blur far away like a cloud, that's all. Wanna hold her, Eddie?

EDDIE: My hands are dirty. (*Sitting up, he is leaning to see the baby.*)

PHIL: 'At's okay. You want her, Mickey?

MICKEY: Sure.

PHIL (*carefully he passes the baby to* MICKEY): She's light as a feather, huh? You can hold her in one hand.

ARTIE: Does she cry?

PHIL: She's very good-natured.

MICKEY: What if she cries?
(MICKEY, *eager to get rid of the baby, moves to pass her to*
EDDIE. PHIL *hastens to the couch, staying protectively
close to the baby, sitting down next to* EDDIE, *as* MICKEY
settles onto the stage left arm of the couch.)

ARTIE: Tell her a joke. (*He is heading up to the counter for the
Burger King bags.*)

EDDIE (*taking the baby*): Ohh, she's real cute. What's hap-
penin', little baby? Makes me miss my kid, huh?

ARTIE: Makes me miss my kid.

MICKEY: I got two of 'em.

EDDIE: This really makes me hate my ex-wife. (EDDIE *laughs a
little, and looks at* MICKEY, *who laughs.*) I mean, I really
hate my ex-wife.
(*Now they start to make jokes, trying to break each
other up, and top each other. All except, of course,* PHIL.)

ARTIE (*having crossed with the bags behind the couch, he
settles on the couch, stage right*): And this little innocent thing here, this sweet little innocent thing is a
broad of the future.

MICKEY: Hard to believe, huh?

EDDIE: Awesome.

ARTIE: Depressing.
(*So they are spread across the couch, from left to right:*
ARTIE, PHIL, EDDIE, MICKEY, *as* ARTIE *starts to hand out
the little packets of French fries.*)

EDDIE: Maybe if we kept her and raised her, she could grow up and be a decent human being.

MICKEY: Unless it's just biologically and genetically inevitable that at a certain age, they go nasty.

PHIL (*reaching to take the baby*): Except for the great ones.

MICKEY: The great ones come along once in a lifetime.

ARTIE: Not in my lifetime.

PHIL (*holding the baby*): Like the terrific athletes of any given generation, there's only a few.

MICKEY (*they are all eating French fries and now the burgers are being passed out*): You think it might be wise or unwise to pay attention to the implications of what we're saying here?

EDDIE: Who has time?

MICKEY: Right. Who has time?

EDDIE: It's hard enough to say what you're sayin', let alone to consider the goddamn implications.

ARTIE: Lemme see her, okay.

PHIL (*as he passes the baby to* ARTIE): We was all that little: each one of us. I'm gonna ask Susie to give me one more try. Just one more. I'm gonna beg her.

MICKEY (*eating*): You oughta call her, Phil; tell her you got the kid, anyway.

PHIL: I'll take the kid back. (*As if he has hit upon a great new idea.*) I'll beg her. I can beg.

EDDIE: Phil, listen to me; you're a rare fuckin' human being. Underneath it all, you got this goddamn potential,
this unbelievable potential. You really do; you could
channel it.

PHIL: I mean, I'm startin' in my car again, Eddie. I was three
days on the highway last week. Three whole days with
nothing but gas station attendants. You know what I'm
sayin', Eddie? (*Suddenly unable to look at* EDDIE, *he
bolts away, crossing toward center near the armchair.*)
I'll beg her. I'll follow her around on my hands and knees
throughout the house. I won't let her out of my sight.
(ARTIE *yelps and stares down at the baby.*)

What happened?

ARTIE (*hurrying to pass the baby to her father*): Yeah, well,
she's a broad already, Phil. Just like every other broad I
ever met, she hadda dump on me. (*As the music, the
harmonica theme, begins very softly.*)

MICKEY: She shit herself?

ARTIE: Yeah. (*Moving to the kitchen for a cloth to wipe his
hand.*)

MICKEY: (*watching as* PHIL *is sinking into the armchair with
the baby*): Look at that smile. She shit herself and look at
that smile.

PHIL (*cradling the baby*): They're very honest. They're very,
very honest.
(*The music builds now quite loud.* ARTIE, *by the counter, has turned to look down.* MICKEY *is leaning on the
couch.* EDDIE *sits on the couch. They all look at* PHIL *and
the baby.*)

CURTAIN

ACT THREE

SCENE 1

Time: Several days later, early evening.

Place: The same.

MICKEY *and* DARLENE *are laughing. They are at the breakfast nook counter,* MICKEY *walking out from behind it carrying a glass of wine while* DARLENE *is seated on the stage left of the two stools sipping her wine. Her jacket lies on the armchair, her purse is on the coffee table.*

MICKEY: All I said was "Has anybody seen him levitate?" So she says to me, "Well, he's an honest person and he has been working at it for years, so if he says he levitates, I see no reason for you to doubt it."

DARLENE: Yeah, Mickey, what are you, a cynic?

MICKEY: I mean, not only is she miffed at me, but the entire room is in sympathy. This is the group consensus: the guy has worked at it, so for asking a question such as "Has anybody seen him levitate?" I'm crude. Or I don't know what.

DARLENE (*tapping his nose with her forefinger*): Bad, bad, bad. (*As* MICKEY *imitates the moans of a guilty dog and grovels, he does not see* EDDIE *come in the front door, carrying a briefcase.* DARLENE'*s back is to* EDDIE.)

Bad, bad.

EDDIE: Bad what?

MICKEY (*startled*): Dog.

DARLENE (*startled but happy to see him*): Hi, honey.

MICKEY: We were talking about that levitation guy, right?

DARLENE (*as she is about to embrace him, he tosses his briefcase onto the couch*): Which led to bad dog. Somehow.

EDDIE: It would have to.

MICKEY: I think it was a logical but almost untraceable sequence of associations.

EDDIE: Been waiting long?
    (MICKEY *and* DARLENE *speak almost simultaneously.*)

DARLENE: No.

MICKEY: Yeah.
    (*They all laugh.*)

I have, she hasn't. I gotta go.

EDDIE (*moving to the phone with* DARLENE *following him*): Phil call?

MICKEY (*moving to the alcove, preparing to leave*): Not that I know of. How's he doin'?

EDDIE: I got a lot of frantic messages at work, and when I tried his house, Susie called me an "asshole" and hung up, and from then on the phone was off the hook. So much for reconciliation.

MICKEY (*making a little joke to* DARLENE): It would appear they've found a pattern to their liking.

DARLENE (*joking to* MICKEY): I mean, Phil's a lot of fun, but on a day-to-day basis, I would have to have a lot of sympathy for Susie.

EDDIE (*making his own joke as he roots through phone messages taken from his pocket*): She's a very sympathetic bitch. That's her staple attribute.

MICKEY (*near the door, he brushes lint from his trousers as* DARLENE, *behind* EDDIE, *hugs him*): You want me to try and hook up with you later, or you up for privacy?

EDDIE: Depends on do I locate Phil or not.

DARLENE: You could call, or we could leave a message.

MICKEY: I'll check my service. See you. (*He goes out the door.*)

EDDIE: Let's just hang around a little in case he calls.

DARLENE (*she is playfully pulling at* EDDIE's *shirt, unbuttoning it*): I'm tired anyway.

EDDIE (*dialing*): It's the kid thing, you know, that's the thing. He could walk in a second it wasn't for the kid.

DARLENE: He should have then.

EDDIE: Exactly. But he couldn't. So what am I talking about? (*Into the phone:*) Hey. Eddie. You heard from Phil? No. No. If you do, call me. I'm at home. Yeah. (*He hangs up and pulls free of her, walks away. Carrying the phone, he moves to the couch, where his briefcase lies.*) It's just a guy like Phil, for all his appearances, this is what can make him nuts. You don't ever forget about 'em if you're a guy like Phil. I mean, my little girl is a factor in every calculation I make—big or small—she's a constant. You can imagine, right? (*Having found a number in his briefcase he dials again.*)

DARLENE (*angry as she moves to sit at the counter near her wine glass and the bottle*): Sure. I had a, you know—and that was—well, rough, so I have some sense of it, really, in a very funny way.

EDDIE (*waiting, the phone to his ear*): What?

DARLENE: My abortion. I got pregnant.
(*He freezes, looks at her.*)

I wasn't sure exactly which guy—I wasn't going crazy or anything with a different guy every night or anything, and I knew them both very well, but I was just not emotionally involved with either one of them, seriously. (*Now, as she pours herself some wine, she has his attention, the phone in his hand but lowered.*)

Though I liked them both. A lot. Which in a way made the whole thing even more confusing on a personal level, and you know, in terms of trying to figure out the morality of the whole thing, so I finally had this abortion completely on my own without telling anybody, not even my girlfriends. I kept thinking in my mind that it wasn't a complete baby, which it wasn't, not a fully developed person, but a fetus, which it was, and then I would have what I would term a real child later, but nevertheless, I felt I had no one to blame but myself, and I went sort of out of my mind for a while, so my parents sent me to Puerto Rico for a vacation, and I got myself back together there enough to come home with my head on my shoulders at least semi-straight. I was functional, anyway. Semi-functional, anyway. But then I told everybody what had happened. I went from telling nobody to everybody.

EDDIE: This was . . .

DARLENE: What?

EDDIE: When?

DARLENE: Seven and a half years ago.

EDDIE: That's what I mean, though; those feelings.

DARLENE: I know. I understood, see, that was what you meant, which was my reason for trying to make the effort to bring it up, because I don't talk about it all that much anymore, but I wanted you to know that when you said that about your daughter, I, in fact in a visceral sense, knew what you were talking about.

EDDIE (*leaving the phone on the coffee table, he moves to her, he embraces her*): I mean, everybody has this baggage, and you can't ignore it or what are you doing?

DARLENE: You're just ignoring it.

EDDIE: You're just ignoring the person. It really messed you up, though, huh?

DARLENE: For a while. But I learned certain things from it, too, you know.

EDDIE (*still holding her*): Sure.

DARLENE: It was painful, you know, but I learned these things that have been a help ever since, so something came out of it good.

EDDIE: So these two guys . . . Where are they?

DARLENE: Oh, I have no idea. This was in Cincinnati.

EDDIE: Did . . . they know each other?

DARLENE: The two guys?

EDDIE: Yeah.

DARLENE: No. I mean, not that I know of. Why?

EDDIE: Just wondering.

DARLENE: What?

EDDIE: Nothing. Just . . . you know.

DARLENE: You must have been wondering something. People don't just wonder nothing.

EDDIE: No, no. I was just wondering, you know, was it a pattern? That's all.

DARLENE: No.

EDDIE: I mean, don't get irritated. You asked me.

DARLENE (*she breaks the embrace, grabs her glass of wine*): I mean, I was trying to tell you something else entirely.

EDDIE: I know that.

DARLENE: So what's the point?

EDDIE: I'm aware absolutely of what you were trying to tell me. And I heard it. But am I just supposed to totally narrow down my whole set of perceptions, just filter out everything, just censor everything that doesn't support your intention? I made an association. And it was not an unreasonable association.

DARLENE (*crossing away to the couch*): It was totally off the wall, and hostile.

EDDIE: Hostile?

DARLENE: And you know it.

EDDIE: Give me a break! What? I'm supposed to sit still for the most arcane association I ever heard in my life, that levitation leads to dogs? But should I come up with an equally—I mean, equally, shit—when I come up with a hundred percent more logical association, I'm supposed to accept your opinion that it isn't?

DARLENE: No, no, no.

EDDIE (*he is moving to her now*): Well, that's all it was. An association. That's all it was.

DARLENE: Okay.

EDDIE (*settling onto the couch beside her*): I mean, for everybody's good, it appeared to me a thought worth some exploration, and if I was wrong, and I misjudged ... (*embracing her*) ... then I'm sorry.

DARLENE: It's just something I'm very, sometimes, sensitive about.

EDDIE: Sure. What? The abortion?

DARLENE (*irritated*): Yeah.

EDDIE (*settling back into the embrace*): Sure. Okay, though? You okay now? You feel okay?

DARLENE (*standing up, she bolts for the kitchen*): I'm hungry. You hungry?

EDDIE: I mean, if we don't talk these things out, we'll just end up with all this, you know, unspoken shit, following us around. (*Following her.*) You wanna go out and eat? Let's go out. What are you hungry for? How about Chinese?

DARLENE: Sure. (*In the kitchen, she is rummaging for something to nibble on.*)

EDDIE (*heading back to the phone, which is on the coffee table*): We could go to Mr. Chou's. Treat ourselves right.

DARLENE: That's great. I love the seaweed. (*Digging open a bag of pretzels.*)

EDDIE: I mean, you want Chinese?

DARLENE: I love Mr. Chou's.

EDDIE: We could go some other place. How about Ma Maison?

DARLENE: Sure.

EDDIE (*running to the Rolodex on the counter*): You like that better than Mr. Chou's?

DARLENE (*increasingly irritated*): It doesn't matter to me.

EDDIE: Which one should I call?

DARLENE: Surprise me.

EDDIE: I don't want to surprise you. I want to, you know, do whatever you really want.

DARLENE: Then just pick one. Call one. Either.

EDDIE: I mean, why should I have to guess? I don't want to guess. Just tell me. I mean, what if I pick the wrong one? (*Heading back to the coffee table and phone.*)

DARLENE: You can't pick the wrong one. Honestly, Eddie, I like them both the same. I like them both exactly the same.

EDDIE (*freezing*): Exactly?

DARLENE: Yes. I like them both.

EDDIE: I mean, how can you possibly think you like them both the same? One is French and one is Chinese. They're different. They're as different as— (*Crossing back to her.*) I mean, what is the world, one big blur to you out there in which everything that bears some resemblance to something else is just automatically put at the same level in your hierarchy, for crissake, Darlene, the only thing they have in common is that THEY'RE BOTH RESTAURANTS!

DARLENE: Are you aware that you're yelling?

EDDIE (*crossing back to the phone*): My voice is raised for emphasis, which is a perfectly legitimate use of volume. Particularly when, in addition, I evidently have to break through this goddamn cloud in which you are obviously enveloped in which everything is just this blur totally devoid of the most rudimentary sort of distinction. (*He is rooting through the Rolodex as she rushes over.*)

DARLENE (*grabbing the phone, she sticks it into his hand*): Just call the restaurant, why don't you?

EDDIE: Why are you doing this?

DARLENE: I'm hungry. I'm just trying to get something to eat before I faint.

EDDIE: The fuck you are. You're up to something.

DARLENE: What do you mean, what am I up to? You're telling me I don't know if I'm hungry or not? I'm hungry!

EDDIE: Bullshit!

DARLENE: "Up to"? Paranoia, Eddie. Para-fucking-noia. Be alert. Your tendencies are coming out all over the place.

EDDIE: I'm fine.

DARLENE: I mean, to stand there screeching at me about what-am-I-up-to is paranoid.

EDDIE: Not if you're up to something it's not.

DARLENE (*storming away toward the counter, the pretzels, the wine*): I'm not. Take my word for it, you're acting a little nuts.

EDDIE: Oh, I'm supposed to trust your judgment of my mental stability? (*He is advancing on her as she pours her wine.*) I'm supposed to trust your evaluation of the nuances of my sanity? You can't even tell the difference between a French and a Chinese restaurant!

DARLENE: I like them both. (*With her wine and pretzels she heads for the couch, flopping down on the stage left end.*)

EDDIE: But they're different! One is French, and the other is Chinese. THEY'RE TOTALLY FUCKING DIFFERENT!

DARLENE: NOT IN MY INNER EMOTIONAL SUBJECTIVE EXPERIENCE OF THEM!

EDDIE (*he moves behind the couch, talking into the back of her head, then around to face her from the stage right side*): The tastes, the decors, the waiters, the accents. The fucking accents. The little phrases the waiters say. And they yell at each other in these whole totally different languages, does none of this make an impression on you?!

DARLENE: It impresses me that I like them both.

EDDIE: Your total inner emotional subjective experience must be THIS EPIC FUCKING FOG! I mean, what are you on, some sort of dualistic trip and everything is in twos and you just can't tell which is which so you're just pulled taut between them on this goddamn high wire between people who might like to have some kind of definitive reaction from you in order to know!

DARLENE: Fuck you!

EDDIE: What's wrong with that?

DARLENE (*leaping up, she turns to leave*): Those two guys. I
   happened to mention two guys!
   (*He grabs her, makes her face him.*)

EDDIE: I just want to know if this is a pattern. Chinese restaurants and you can't tell the difference between people!
   (*They stand, staring at each other.*)

DARLENE: Oh, Eddie. Oh, Eddie, Eddie.

EDDIE: What?

DARLENE: Oh, Eddie, Eddie. (*Moving to the armchair, she
   slumps down, her back to him.*)

EDDIE: What?

DARLENE: I just really feel awful. This is really depressing. I
   really like you. I really do.

EDDIE: I mean . . .

DARLENE: What?

EDDIE: Well, don't feel too bad, okay?

DARLENE: I do, I feel bad. I feel bad.

EDDIE (*now, he sits on the edge of the couch, and leans toward
   her*): But, I mean, just—we have to talk about these
   things, right? That's all. This is okay.

DARLENE: No, no.

EDDIE: Just don't—you know, on the basis of this, make any
   sort of grand, kind of overwhelming, comprehensive,
   kind of, you know, totally conclusive assessment here.

That would be absurd, you know. I mean, this is an isolated, individual thing here, and—

DARLENE: No.

EDDIE (*moving to the chair, he tries to get close to her, settles on his knees on the floor*): Sure. I mean, sometimes what is it? It's stuff, other stuff; stuff under stuff, you're doing one thing you think it's something else. I mean, it's always there, the family thing, the childhood thing, it's—sometimes it comes up. I go off. (*And he really has gone off. He is a man coming back.*) I'm not even where I seem anymore. I'm not there.

DARLENE: Eddie, I think I should go.

EDDIE: I'm trying to explain.

DARLENE (*sliding away from him, she moves to the couch and her purse on the coffee table*): I know all about it.

EDDIE: Whata you know all about?

DARLENE: Your fucking childhood, Eddie. You tol' me.

EDDIE: Whata you know?

DARLENE (*she rummages through her purse, looking for something*): I know all I—what is this, a test? I mean, I know: your parents were these religious lunatics, these pious frauds, who periodically beat the shit out of you.

EDDIE: They weren't just religious, and they didn't just—

DARLENE: Your father was a minister, I know.

EDDIE: What denomination?

DARLENE: Fuck you. (*She bolts away to the armchair, where her jacket hangs on the back.*)

EDDIE: You said you knew.

DARLENE: I don't think there's a lot more we ought to, with any, you know, honesty, allow ourselves in the way of bullshit about our backgrounds to exonerate what is our just plain mean behavior to one another.

EDDIE: That's not what I'm doing.

DARLENE: So, what are you doing?

EDDIE (*following her*): They took me in the woods; they prayed and then they beat the shit out of me; they prayed and beat me with sticks. He talked in tongues.

DARLENE: She broke your nose and blacked your eyes, I know. (*The phone, lying on the coffee table, rings.*)

EDDIE: Because I wanted to watch *Range Rider* on TV and she considered it a violent program.
(*The phone rings.*)

So she broke my nose. That's insane. (*As he steps in the direction of the phone.*)

DARLENE (*bolting for the door*): But I don't care, Eddie. I don't care.

EDDIE (*he grabs her by the arm to detain her*): It doesn't matter? What are you talking about? (*Dragging her down toward the phone.*)

Darlene: It doesn't.

Eddie: No, no, no. (*Snatching up the phone, he yells into it.*) Hold on! (*Clutching* Darlene, *the phone pressed against his chest, he faces her.*) No, no; it matters, and you care. What you mean is, it doesn't make any difference! (*Releasing her, he turns to the phone.*) Hello.

Darlene: I can't stand this goddamn semantic insanity anymore, Eddie—I can't be that specific about my feelings—I can't. Will you get off the phone!?

Eddie (*into the phone*): What? Oh, no. No, no. Oh, no.

Darlene: What?

Eddie (*into phone*): Wait there. There. I'll come over. (*He drops the phone onto the couch.*)

Darlene: Eddie, what? You look terrible. What?
(Eddie, *in a daze, looks at her, then starts toward the door.*)

Eddie, who was that? What happened? Eddie!

Eddie: Phil's dead.

Darlene: What?

Eddie: Car. Car.

Darlene: Oh, Eddie, Eddie.

Eddie: What?

(EDDIE *goes, and as he leaves her alone in the room, "Unchained Melody" sung by Willie Nelson starts, this time starting at the very beginning.* DARLENE *is there, the lights fading.*)

BLACKOUT

(*The music continues.*)

SCENE 2

Time: Several days later. Evening.

Place: The same.

In the dark "Unchained Melody" continues. ARTIE, *dressed in a dark suit, enters, turning on the lights by the door. He looks about, then walks to the kitchen as* EDDIE *enters, carrying* PHIL's *jacket and the day's mail, envelopes and magazines, the* TV Guide. *In the kitchen* ARTIE *checks the coffee pot as* EDDIE *hangs* PHIL's *coat on the hook on the support beam near the front door where* PHIL *has always hung his coat. As he's doing this,* MICKEY *comes in, taking off his own jacket, which he hangs on the closet door as* EDDIE *crosses to the kitchen and* MICKEY, *peeling an orange, crosses down to the couch and sits, his feet up on the coffee table, and the music fades out.*

ARTIE (*looking from* MICKEY *to* EDDIE): So now what?

MICKEY: I'm beat. What's his name, his agent, wasn't there. You see him?

ARTIE (*with his coffee cup, he moves toward* MICKEY): He's an asshole. He probably would have gone berserk to be at Phil's funeral. I was almost berserk.

MICKEY: So it was just as well he didn't come.

ARTIE: Fuck him. There's no excuse.

MICKEY (*eating his orange*): Funerals aren't for everybody. As Phil demonstrated. Life wasn't for him.

ARTIE (*sitting on the arm of the couch*): You think he meant it?

MICKEY: As much as he meant anything. How you doin'?

ARTIE (*quite agitated*): I'm okay. Except I feel, though, somewhat like at any moment I could turn into a hysterical like, you know . . . rabbit.

MICKEY: Yeah. What would that be like?

ARTIE: I think I'm gonna go home. (*Moving away from* MICKEY.) I think I'm gonna go home, Eddie. What time is it? I'm whipped.

MICKEY: Ten twenty . . . two.

ARTIE: Ten? Ten? It feels like goddamn four in the morning. I feel like I been awake for years.

MICKEY: It's ten twenty-two.

ARTIE: It is, isn't it. My watch is stopped. What happened to my watch? I'm whipped. (*At the counter, he is hoping for* EDDIE's *attention.*) It takes it out of you, huh, Eddie, a day like this?

MICKEY: Death . . . takes it out of you?

ARTIE: Yeah.

EDDIE: What you gonna do tomorrow?

ARTIE: I got a bunch of meetings. We got a development deal.

EDDIE: Yeah? (*Moving to* ARTIE.)

ARTIE: Set, too. On paper. Good terms; very good terms. Terms I'm totally overjoyed about.
(*There is an echo in this of their first scene:* ARTIE *is aggressive and positive here; he is not going to let* EDDIE *get at him again.*)

EDDIE (*he gives* ARTIE *a hug*): Come by, okay?

ARTIE: Sure. Late. (*Starting for the door.*)

EDDIE: Whatever.

ARTIE: Take care, you guys.

MICKEY: You, too, Artie. Fuck him, huh?

ARTIE: (*at the door,* ARTIE *hesitates*): The jerk-off. (*He goes.*)

MICKEY (MICKEY, *cleaning up a little, crosses with an ashtray to the waste can, as* EDDIE, *with the mail, moves down to the armchair to sit*): How you doin', Edward?

EDDIE (*putting on his glasses to read the mail*): I don't know. You?

MICKEY (*dumping the ashtray*): Okay.

EDDIE: Oh, I'm okay. I mean, I'm okay. Is that what you're askin'?

MICKEY: Yeah.

EDDIE: Yeah, shit. I'm okay.

MICKEY: Good.
    (*As* MICKEY *climbs the stairs,* EDDIE *freezes staring at a letter.*)

EDDIE: Holy Jesus holy Christ, I got a letter. Phil. Phil.

MICKEY: What?

EDDIE (*tearing open the letter*): Yeah!

MICKEY: What's it say? (*Coming down to the landing rail to stare at* EDDIE.)

EDDIE: What? WHAT? It's postmarked on the day—he mailed it on the day. (*Unfolding the letter.*) "The guy who dies in an accident understands the nature of destiny. Phil."

MICKEY: What? (*As* EDDIE *comes running up to hand the letter to* MICKEY.)

EDDIE: That's what it says.

MICKEY: "The guy who dies in an accident understands the nature of destiny"?

EDDIE: To die in—what the fuck? I mean, Mickey, what, what, what?

MICKEY (*with a shrug*): It's a fucking fortune cookie. (*He hands the letter back to* EDDIE *and starts up the stairs.*)

EDDIE: I mean, if he killed himself, this is the note.

MICKEY: Whata you mean "if"?

EDDIE: I'm giving him the benefit of the doubt. (*Returning to the armchair to intently study the letter, as* MICKEY *turns back on the stairs.*)

MICKEY: Eddie, c'mon, you wanna look this thing in the eye. You don't do a hundred down that narrow crease in the high ground because you're anxious to get home. A hundred MPH down Mulholland on a star-filled night is not the way to longevity. The guy behaved often, and finally, like some, you know, soulful jerk-off. Fuck him and forget him. What more can I say.

EDDIE: I'm gonna look up the words. (*Running for the record player where he expects to find the dictionary.*)

MICKEY: What?

EDDIE: On the thing here, I'm gonna see if the dictionary might help. (*But he can't find the dictionary.*)

MICKEY: Look up the words? Are you out of your mind? Don't get involved in this thing. Don't waste your time.

EDDIE: But this is it—this is what he wanted to tell us. (*Running up the stairs past* MICKEY, EDDIE *waves the note and heads into his room.*)

MICKEY (*on the stairs*): He had somethin' to say he could a give us a phone call; he could have stopped by; our door was open. He wants to get some information to me now, he's going to have to bridge the gap directly; he's going to have to make an appearance, difficult as it might be. (EDDIE, *with the dictionary, comes out of the bedroom as* MICKEY *seeks to block* EDDIE's *descent; he takes the dictionary from* EDDIE's *hands.*)

Listen to me: Stay away from this shit. He's dead: He didn't want to discuss it before, I don't want to discuss it after.

EDDIE (*taking the dictionary back*): But that's exactly what I'm talking about—that this is a clue. To something. Maybe why. (*He sits on the stairs to start looking up the words.*) I want to know why.

MICKEY: What why? There's no why in a disaster like this. You know, the earth moved. He was in the wrong place; this big hole opens up, what's he gonna do? (*He drops off the stairs, heading into the kitchen for something to eat.*)

EDDIE: Your attitude, Mickey—will you please examine your fucking attitude?

MICKEY: This is a dead end is all I'm saying. There's no traffic with this thing. You go in, you don't come out. The guy made a decision beyond communication.

EDDIE (*waving the note through the rungs of the banister at* MICKEY): He left a note.

MICKEY (*snatching the note*): The note is tangential. It's part of his goof, you know, that he was a rational human being, when he wasn't. I want no part of this fucking beyond-the-grave extension of his jerk-off sensibility.

EDDIE (*having run down with the dictionary, he is after the note, but* MICKEY *disdainfully drops it on the counter*): The note is what he wanted us to think.

MICKEY (*pulling a small carton of apple juice from the refrigerator*): Bullshit.

EDDIE (*smoothing the note out on the counter*): He left it. (*He sits on the stage left stool with his dictionary and note on the counter.*)

MICKEY: To drive us nuts from long distance. Lemme see that— (*As* MICKEY *reaches for the note,* EDDIE *presses his hand down on the note, protectively.*) What is this?

EDDIE: I'm gonna look up the words.

MICKEY: It's a fucking fortune cookie. (*Sipping his juice through a straw, he sneaks up on the note, his back along the front of the counter.*) What's to look up? (*Leaning back, he can read it.*) "A guy who." That's him. (*Turning the note with his finger.*) "Dies." In case we didn't know, he gave us a demonstration. (*Now he gently picks the note up.*) "Accident" is to propel yourself into a brief but unsustainable orbit, and then attempt to land in a tree on the side of a cliff-like incline. (*Hopping up to sit on the counter.*) "Understand" is what he had no part of. "Nature" is the tree, and "destiny" is, if you're him, you're an asshole.

EDDIE (*leaving the note with* MICKEY, EDDIE *crosses down to the armchair to examine the envelope*): Look. Count the letters.

MICKEY: What?

EDDIE (*he is working with the dictionary*): Count the words and the letters, I want to know how many letters.

MICKEY (*hopping down, moving toward* EDDIE): Eddie, this is dementia, here. You've flipped a circuit. Grief has put you out of order.

EDDIE: You never heard of an anagram?

MICKEY: Sure.

EDDIE: So maybe it's an anagram.

MICKEY: You think this is an anagram? (*Now he veers off toward the couch.*)

EDDIE: You don't have to have any faith in the fucking thought, but just as a favor, you know, participate, okay. Help me move it along. That's all I'm asking. (*As* MICKEY *sits.*) And keep your sarcasm to yourself.

MICKEY: What sarcasm?

EDDIE (*trying to concentrate on the dictionary*): Can you do that?

MICKEY: What sarcasm? I'm—you know—this is— What sarcasm? This is insulting.

EDDIE: You're getting sidetracked.

MICKEY: I'll do this goddamn lunacy. I'll count the letters here, but get one thing straight, all right? There's no sarcasm here. (*Throwing the note down on the coffee table, he storms to the kitchen to pour himself a drink.*)

I've indulged in nothing even remotely sarcastic here, and I want that understood because you have obviously not understood it. So I'll make allowances, but if I've been flip, it's to put some humor into what could be totally and utterly morbid—and there have been times in the goddamn history of mankind where a little humor won a person some affection for the effort, you know, not to go under; anybody can go under. (*Having poured a drink, he now is so agitated, he knocks it over.*) I mean, we're all goin' fucking under, so how about a little laugh along the way? So I'm flip. So what!

EDDIE: I don't feel like being flip, Mickey.

MICKEY: Right. But you wanna do an anagram on his death note, right?!

EDDIE: "Flip" IS "sarcastic," Mickey.

MICKEY: It is not. It's—"flip." It's on a whole other level, a whole other lower level and just lighter.

EDDIE: To me, it's "sarcastic."

MICKEY: But that's crazy! Sarcastic is "heavy." It's mean. Funny, sure, but mean. I do both, but this was flip.

EDDIE: You shoulda heard yourself.

MICKEY (*crossing back behind* EDDIE *to the couch*): I did.

EDDIE: You shoulda listened closer.

MICKEY (*snatching the note up from the coffee table, he flops down with a pencil*): You wanna get on with this.

EDDIE (*rising with the dictionary, he paces thoughtfully*

about): So I have "accident" here, and "destiny." "Accident: a happening that is not expected, foreseen or intended. Two, an unfortunate occurrence or mishap, sudden fall, collision, usually resulting in physical injury." Blah-blah, just repeats basically. And "destiny," we have, "The inevitable or necessary succession of events. What will necessarily happen to any person or thing." So . . . (*with a sense of discovery, he moves toward* MICKEY *on the couch*) . . . if you die in a happening that is not expected, foreseen or intended, you understand the inevitable or necessary succession of events.

MICKEY: Fuck him.

EDDIE: It makes sense! (*Triumphant, grabbing the note from* MICKEY.)

MICKEY: It makes no sense.

EDDIE: I mean, we owe him to understand as best we can what he wanted. Nobody has to believe it. IT MAKES FUCKING SENSE.

MICKEY (*emphatically*): Anyway, he did it on purpose so it was no goddamn accident. And if it was no accident, then his note is categorically, definitively irrelevant.
(*And for both of them it seems that* MICKEY *has made the winning point.* EDDIE, *dejected, sits there, taking off his glasses.*)

EDDIE: But how did he get there? Exactly how did he get to that point where in his own mind he could do it on purpose? That's what—

MICKEY: It's not that big a deal—that's the fucking truth, you know, you make an adjustment, that's all—you shift your point of view a little and what was horrible looks okay. (*He gently takes the note from* Eddie.) All the necessary information that might deter you gets locked away. (*With relish.*) Little gremlins divert the good thoughts so you don't hear them. You just hear the bad thoughts, which at this point are convincing you they're a good idea. (*Rising, his relish increasing, he loosens his tie, moving toward the kitchen, where he will get some Häagen-Dazs ice cream from the refrigerator.*) You get an idea, that's all. You don't understand the scope of it; you just lose the scope of it. So there you are, foot's on the gas, you're flying. So far so good. No big deal. Road, trees, radio. What's a little flick of the steering wheel? Maybe an inch's rotation. Nothing to it. An inch, what's that? So you do it. (*Eating the ice cream, he stands behind the counter, his enjoyment of his ideas, his own cleverness growing.*) But with that, what? You've gone beyond what you can come back from. You've handed control over now, it's gravity and this big machine, which is a car, who are in charge now. Only it's not a car anymore! (*Really enjoying himself, as he crumples the note.*) It's this hunk of metal rearranging itself according to the laws of physics, force and reaction, stress and resistance; heat, friction, collapse, and then you're gone. (*Happily tossing the note into the waste can.*) Who knows where.

EDDIE (*crossing, he retrieves the note*): So how many letters?

MICKEY: Right. The fucking anagram. This is exciting, Eddie; I've never been involved with a being from another planet before. Twelve and fifty-four. (*He starts rooting around in the shelves, looking for something.*)

EDDIE: Twelve words and fifty-four letters. That's interesting.

MICKEY: It's interesting, huh?

EDDIE: I mean, twelve is one and two which are three; and fifty-four is five and four: that's nine, or three squared. There's lots of relationships.

MICKEY (*adding chocolate chips by the spoonful onto his ice cream*): I never thought of all that.

EDDIE (*pacing, looking at the note*): I tried to warn him, you know. She was a snake. And I tried to tell him, you know, she was out to absolutely undermine the little faith he had in himself. I saw it coming; she hadda see it coming. I mean, for all his toughness, he was made out of thin air, he was a pane of glass, and if you went near him, you knew it. I'm gonna call her. (*Storming to the stage left side of the counter to grab the phone.*)

MICKEY: Who? Susie? (*Inside the nook, he tries to stop him.*) Eddie, you don't know what you're doing. You can't call her up in the middle of the night; she's a widow. She just put her husband in the ground.

EDDIE (*tearing free of* MICKEY, *he lunges backward*): I want her to have some fucking cognizance of this event.

MICKEY: She knows.

EDDIE: She killed him? You ain't sayin' she's looking at it from the context she killed him?

MICKEY: What?

EDDIE: You bet you're not because what she knows is he's dead and that's how much better than him she is. No more teddy bears—she's takin' care of business, so she's a together bitch, and he's weak, he punked out. A person cannot keep up their self-respect they know they look like some goddamn crazed insensitive prick who goes around dropping kids out of his life like they're trash to him. I saw it in him. She should have. What the hell was she thinking about?

MICKEY (*as* MICKEY, *advancing on* EDDIE, *seems about to take the phone*): Herself. I don't know. What do people think about?

EDDIE (*hurling the phone*): Fuck her. What's she got to think about?

MICKEY (*fleeing back into the nook, he begins digging things out from the shelves behind the counter: a jar of honey, bag of chips and then the dope box*): She wanted things. I don't know. So she thought about the things she wanted. You want to kill her for what she was doing—to get the things she wanted? (*As the dope box hits the counter,* EDDIE *grabs it.*) You can't kill people for that.

EDDIE: She killed him.

MICKEY: You're gonna die a this shit, Eddie. Does it not cross your mind?

EDDIE: Hey, don't get serious here, Mickey. You know, don't get morbid here and ruin a nice evening. Die of it is a little extreme. You have to admit that. (*Grabbing a vial, he darts to the couch and coffee table on which he spreads coke.*) And even if it isn't, take care of myself for what? For some state-of-the-art bitch to get her hooks into me. They're fucking ghouls, Mickey. They eat our hearts.

MICKEY: You don't know what you're saying. You don't. (*Pouring a large glass of vodka.*)

EDDIE: I do.

MICKEY (*he crosses to the armchair, sits*): I know what you think you're saying, but you're not saying it.

EDDIE: I do. I do. I know what I'm saying. I don't know what I mean, but I know what I'm saying. Is that what you mean?

MICKEY: Yeah. (*Picking up the TV remote.*)

EDDIE: Right. But who knows what anything means, though, huh? It's not like anybody knows that, so at least I know I don't know, which is more than most people. They probably think they know what they mean, not just what they think they mean. You feel that, Mickey, huh? (*As* MICKEY *turns on the TV,* EDDIE *does a line of coke off the coffee table.*) About death, that when it comes, you're just going along in this goddamn ongoing inner rapateta, rapateta, blah-blah-blah, in which you understand this or that, and tell yourself about it, and then you ricochet on, and then it just cuts out mid-something. Mid-realization. "Oh, now I under—" Blam! You're gone. Wham! Comatose. Dead. You think that's how it is? (*Face to face with* MICKEY, *very close to him.*)

MICKEY: I'm going to bed. (*Turning off the TV.*) And you should, too. Go to bed. You're a mess. Phil would want you to get your rest. (*He crosses to the kitchen.*)

EDDIE (*following* MICKEY): Fuck you about him, Mickey! I mean, where do you get the goddamn cynicism, the goddamn scorn to speak his name, let alone—

MICKEY (*as he is loading the vodka bottle, a glass, some chips, some soda, some ice cream, some honey into a large wooden bowl*): Eddie, Eddie, is everything my fault?

EDDIE: What'd you ever do but mock him and put him down?

MICKEY: Relent, I beg you.

EDDIE: You ain't saying you ever did one good thing for him, are you, not one helpful thing!?

MICKEY (*heading with his supplies for the stairs*): No, Eddie, what I'm saying is that unlike you, I never lied to him.

EDDIE: And you never loved him either.

MICKEY (*pausing before the stairway to gloat*): Right, Eddie. Good taste has no doubt deprived me of a great many things.

EDDIE: You lie to yourself, Mickey.

MICKEY: Who better? (*Stepping toward the stairs as* EDDIE *leaps in front of him.*)

EDDIE: No guts. No originality; no guts.
(*Shoving* MICKEY *back,* EDDIE *sits on the steps.*)

MICKEY (*pacing about, clutching his bowl of supplies*): You want this goddamn ultra-modern, post-hip, comprehensive, totally fucking cost-efficient explanation of everything by which you uncover the preceding events which determined the following events, but you're not gonna find it.

EDDIE: SAYS YOU!

MICKEY (*advancing on* EDDIE, *who sits on the steps doing a line of coke off his hand*): You wanna believe that if you do or don't do certain things now, certain other things will or won't happen down the road, accordingly. You

think you're gonna parlay this finely tuned circuitry you
have for a brain into some form of major participation in
the divine conglomerate, man, but all you're gonna
really do is make yourself and everyone around you,
nuts.

EDDIE *(leaping up)*: HEY! HEY! I'm just tryin' to level out
here, you know. Get this operation into cruise. *(He backs
MICKEY up.)* I mean, I know I gotta cool out but not
tonight. I mean, NOT TONIGHT. *(MICKEY tries to get
around the front of the couch and head for the stairs,
but EDDIE blocks his way.)* I got a history lecture in
progress, you know—the lobes are humming—I'm picking up everything—the radar screens are in full rotation,
they're picking up the coast-to-coast flights. Phil is
sending me messages, you know. He's got complaints
about the great beyond! *(Shaking a little from the drugs,
he rushes to grab PHIL's coat from off the hook under the
balcony.)* I got sonar bouncing off the moon, and
memories—arguments with past and present. I need
somethin' to cut the levels of the distortion, you know. I
need somethin' to modulate the volume. *(Wildly, putting on PHIL's coat, he has backed MICKEY up against
the TV.)*

MICKEY: I mean, to whatever extent THIS FUCKING TOR-
MENT OF YOURS is over whatshername, Darlene, believe me, she isn't worth it.

EDDIE *(taken aback, he retreats to the couch)*: Ohhh, that
move you made when you gave her up for her own good,
that was genius. Whatever prayer I might have had was
gone. She had you down as some form of totally unique,
altruistic phenomenon, instead of the fact that you had a
low opinion of her and what you really wanted was to
fuck the bubble-brain Artie had brought to us.

MICKEY: So what? (*Heading for the stairs, carrying his bowl of supplies.*)

EDDIE: You're no better off than me.

MICKEY: Just slightly.

EDDIE: You don't have any feelings at all.

MICKEY: I don't have your feelings, Eddie; that's all. I have my own. They get me by.

EDDIE: So what kind of friendship is this?

MICKEY: Adequate. Good night. (*Turning, he climbs the stairs.*)

EDDIE: Somethin' terrible is goin' on, Mickey. It's a dark time.

MICKEY: People been sayin' that since the beginning of time, Eddie. Don't feel particularly put upon, okay. Forget about it.

EDDIE: That doesn't mean forget about it. That just means it's been going on a long time. (*Leaping to his feet.*) C'mon, stay up with me—we'll rant at the tube!

MICKEY (*at the top of the stairs, he doesn't even look down*): No, I'm sleepy.

EDDIE: C'mon, Mickey!

MICKEY: No, I'm beat. (*Turning, looking down over the balcony.*) Wait up for Phil, why don't you? Wouldn't that be great, if Phil came by to keep you company?! I'm sure he will.

EDDIE: FUCK YOU! C'MON!

MICKEY (*crossing to his door*): Good night.

EDDIE (*running around looking for the TV remote*): The tube, the tube—it's the asshole of our times. You'll love it. (MICKEY'S *door slams and* EDDIE, *having found the remote, turns on the TV and there is the Johnny Carson music.*) FUCK YOU MICKEY! All right. All right. I'm on my own. (*He starts talking to Johnny Carson on the TV.*) How you doin', huh, John? (*Rushing to the counter, he grabs booze bottles, coke, vials of pills.*) Hey, Carson! Hey, you motherfucker, huh? It's you and me, that's right. Head to head. Eyeball to eyeball, John. And I am fortified. (*Wild, he holds up his various drugs and vials.*) Here's for my left lobe. Here's for my right lobe. And here's to keep the spark plugs blasting. (*From the TV, the audience is shouting "Yo" to Johnny.*) Yo! Yo! (*Johnny announces that this is* The Tonight Show's *nineteenth anniversary.*) Your anniversary! (*Running to set his supplies on the coffee table, he drops onto the floor at the end of the coffee table so he faces the TV.*) Oh, my God. Your anniversary! No, you didn't get my card because I didn't send you a fucking card. John! (*And he does a line of coke as the audience laughs.*) You think that's funny? Bullshit! Funny is your friends disappearing down roads and behind closed doors. We got a skull in our skin, John, and we got ghosts. That's funny. (*Rooting around in the pocket of* PHIL'S *jacket, which he still wears, he pulls out* PHIL'S *silver chrome-plated pistol, which we saw in the first scene. Johnny says something about "foreplay."*) Foreplay? Foreplay? (*Holding the gun awkwardly, he sets it on the coffee table, staring at it.*) Grow up! They're talking about quarks. They want us to think about quarks. They're going to teach our children about quarks. And black holes. Imagine that. Black holes, John. The heavens. Astronauts. Men in—OH! (*Suddenly re-*

*membering, rooting in a newspaper lying on top of
the coffee table.)* This morning, John, there was
this guy— Oh, you want funny? This one'll put you
away, John— We got this guy on the obit page—he
WAS an astronaut, who went round the moon and
ended up in Congress and had surgery for a malignancy
in his nose, then passed away six months later. *(He now
finds the page.)* I know, I know, it's touchy material,
John, but it's rich, it's ripe, you'll love it. His campaign
slogan was, "I was privileged to be one of the few who
viewed our earth from the moon, and that vision taught
me that technology and commitment can overcome
any challenge." Here's a guy who went into orbit; he
rendezvoused with the moon, and from that vantage
what most impressed him was HIS OWN ABILITY TO
GET THERE! Hovering in the heavens, what he saw
was the MAGNIFICENCE OF MEN AND MACHINES!
HE MIGHT AS WELL HAVE BEEN IN DETROIT.
Right? And if technology and commitment are the in-
struments to overcome any challenge, I want to ask
him, what about his nose?! *(Yammering from the TV.)* I
know, I know. *(Grabbing the gun, he retreats as if in
shame, scooting backward, half crawling.)* I could have
crossed the boundary here of discretion. It's possible:
my own sense of discrimination has taken quite a blast.
I've been humbled, John. *(Clutching the pistol, looking
at it.)* I been blasted. And I mean, I'm not tryin' to make
a finished thing here, just rough in a couple of
ideas. You could refine 'em, put your stable on 'em.
Right? Right, John? You're not listening to me. *(At the
chair and hassock, he lies on his side, facing out, rais-
ing the pistol to his head.)* You never listen to me. You
never listen to me. *(As the door opens and* DONNA *steps
in, dressed differently, but similarly, and carrying her
bag, she peeks in, steps in. She cannot see* EDDIE's *head
or the pistol, her view blocked by the chair and hassock.)*

DONNA: Hey, Eddie!
(*Startled, he freezes.*)

I ain't mad anymore. You mad? (*Slowly, she advances toward him, hoping to say something that will entertain him, as he slips the gun back into the pocket of the jacket.*) See my, ah, you know, outfit? I got a little bit from everywhere I been so I'm like my own, you know, whatchamacallit. Right? Bits and pieces. So you can look at me and get the whole picture. See—here's Vermont. (*She is pointing to patches on her jacket.*) Which is a New England state. So if you put it together with a little thought, you can see I hitchhiked up and down the entire East Coast.

EDDIE (*he lies there, looking up at her*): Unless you took a plane.

DONNA: Oh, no. I didn't. Airplane? Where would I get the money? How you been?

EDDIE: I'm a wreck.

DONNA (*looking down at him*): You look a wreck, actually, but I didn't want to be impolite and mention it.

EDDIE: I don't know what I'm doing, you know what I mean? (*He is like a lost child.*)

DONNA: You're watchin' TV.

EDDIE: Right. (*He looks at the TV.*)

DONNA (*she is peeking about for something; she is edging toward the kitchen*): I'm gonna eat something, okay?

EDDIE (*turning off the TV with the remote*): I don't know when I thought of you last, and in you walk. I don't get it.

DONNA: I'm a surprise is all.

EDDIE: But I mean, I don't know what pertains to me and what doesn't. (*Getting to his feet, he pursues her with great urgency.*)

DONNA: Whata you mean?

EDDIE (*following her to the counter*): I mean, everything. Right? I don't know what of everything going on pertains to me and what is of no account at all.

DONNA (*putting Cheerios in a bowl*): Everything pertains to you, Eddie.

EDDIE: Yeah?

DONNA: Sure. It's all part of the flow of which we are a part, too, and everything pertains to everything one way or another, see what I mean?

EDDIE (*desperate*): But I don't know, see, I don't KNOW.

DONNA: It doesn't matter.

EDDIE (*intent upon her, staying very close to her*): So I'm just in this flow, right, like you in your elevator.

DONNA (*having poured milk, she's eating*): It wasn't mine.

EDDIE: So how'm I supposed to feel about it? See that's what I don't know.

DONNA: You have total, utter, complete freedom on that score, Eddie, because it doesn't make a bit of difference.

EDDIE: What I feel, it doesn't matter? This flow don't care!

DONNA: I don't think so.

EDDIE: So fuck it then! What good is it? (*Angrily despairing as he paces away.*)

DONNA: I don't know.

EDDIE: Wait a minute, wait a minute—I don't think you know what I'm talking about. And I'm trying to grasp and, you know, incorporate as good advice what is your basic and total misunderstanding. I mean, is it pertinent, for example, that you came by?

DONNA: It doesn't matter.

EDDIE: I know that's what you think, but that's only because you have totally missed my point.

DONNA: Oh, no. So what is it?

EDDIE: I'm trying to say.

DONNA: Great!

EDDIE: I HAVE SO MUCH TO FIGURE OUT. (*Near the TV, he grabs up the newspaper as the drugs hit him again and he is sick from them, shaking and cold from them, huddling in his jacket.*) I mean, there's you there, and there's other items like this and does it pertain to me, FOR EXAMPLE, that I read that my-government-is-selling-baby-milk-formula-to-foreign-countries-in-order-that-the-mothers'-milk-will-dry-up-from-lack-of-use-and-the-formula-supply—you following me so far? (*Handing her the paper, he paces in front of her, pounding the counter—grieving, shaking with chills and huddling in* PHIL'S *jacket—almost as if he is himself these babies.*)—the-formula-supply-is-cut-off-and-the-babies-starve. I mean, how am I supposed to feel about that? First of all, I can't even be certain that it's true. All I can be sure of is that it's printed in this goddamn newspaper. And I can't find out. How'm I supposed to find out? Write my congressman? Hire a goddamn private detective? Bring my private life to a screeching halt and look into it? And should I ever figure it out, how the hell do I influence the course of these things? I mean, they're not going to put it on the ballot—PROPOSITION 39—Do you favor starving children in a foreign land? I mean, what am I supposed to do about all these things?

DONNA: I don't know.

EDDIE: That's my point, that's what I'm saying.

DONNA: So I do know your point.

EDDIE: But do they pertain to me?

DONNA: You're certainly worried about them.

EDDIE (*frustrated, he paces away*): I AM AWARE THAT I'M WORRIED ABOUT THEM!

DONNA (*moving after him, carrying her knapsack*): I mean, I was saying to you that they all pertain to you as much as they're part of everything, right? That's what I was saying.

EDDIE: But as real things or as rumors?

DONNA: Whichever they are.

EDDIE: Which we don't know.
(*Downstage of the armchair, they face each other near the hassock.*)

DONNA: Right. So this would qualify as a mystery, Eddie, right?

EDDIE: Yeah.

DONNA (*patting his arm*): So you can't straighten out a mystery, right? That's all I'm saying.
(EDDIE *stares at her.*)

EDDIE: Did you know Phil is dead? (*He sits on the coffee table facing out.*)

DONNA: Wow. What happened? (*Settling down on the edge of the hassock, looking at him.*)

EDDIE: He drove his car off Mulholland.

DONNA: What happened?

EDDIE: The car crashed.

DONNA: No shit. I read about that. (*Dropping the knapsack, she wildly roots through the paper.*) I read about that in the paper, but I didn't recognize his name, even though it was the same name.

EDDIE: Funeral was today.

DONNA (*she drops the paper, looks at him*): Wow. So that's why you're such a wreck, Eddie. No wonder. (*Moving to him, she kneels on the floor beside him.*) You were at the funeral.

EDDIE: Yeah.

DONNA: That'd wreck anybody.

EDDIE: Yeah.

DONNA: Was it sad? (*She takes his hand.*)

EDDIE (*with a shrug,* EDDIE, *in his bitterness, doesn't seem to care at all*): You know, everybody wears the suits, you do the things. Everybody's there; you hang around, you know. The cars. Everybody gets to the church. So the priest is there, he blah-blah-blah, some guy is singing, mmmmmmmmmmmmmmnnnnnnnnnn, you drive to the cemetery, right. Everybody's in a line, cars all in a line. Brrrmmmm, brrrrrrmmmm. Everybody's in the cars; blah-blah, blah-blah-blah. So we get to the cemetery, the priest's got some more to say, rapateta, rapateta. So there's the hole, put him in. Blah-blah, blah-blah-blah.

DONNA: Was it sad? (*She squeezes his hand.*)

EDDIE: There was in the church we were all like a bunch of dogs. This guy would sing with his beautiful voice. He had this beautiful high voice. All alone. No organ or anything. Just his voice. And we would all start to cry. The priest could say anything, a lot of nice things; sad things. Nothin'. But then this guy from way in the back of the church would sing, and you couldn't hear the words even, just this high, beautiful, sad sound, this human sound, and we would all start to cry along with him. (*Somewhere here it hits him, a grief that, though there are tears, is beyond them: It is in his body, which heaves, and wracks him.*)

DONNA (*she pats him*): You know somethin', Eddie. I didn't really go to all these places on my clothes.

EDDIE: No.

DONNA: I thought about them all though and bought the souvenirs at a local souvenir place, and I dreamed these big elaborate dreams, but actually I went out of here north toward San Francisco, but I got no farther than Oxnard.

EDDIE (*sitting up, trying to get himself under control*): I know where Oxnard is.

DONNA (*with immense enthusiasm, incredible happiness*): Great!

EDDIE (*laughing a little*): What's so great about me knowing where Oxnard is?

DONNA: It's great when people know what each other are talking about, right, isn't that what we been talking about? I fell in love with a Mexican there. But after a while it wasn't love.

EDDIE: What was it?

DONNA: A mess. So I'm gonna sleep here if you don't mind. You got room?

EDDIE (*rising, he paces for the door*): I'm gonna be up for a while.

DONNA: That's okay; should I lay down on the floor?

EDDIE: No, there's room here. (*Indicating the couch.*) You can sleep here. (*He is hanging* PHIL'*s coat on the hook on the beam.*)

DONNA: Great. (*Moving with her knapsack to the couch.*)

EDDIE: I don't know if I'm going to sleep ever again. I might stay awake forever. (*He is up by the door, looking out.*)

DONNA: That's okay. I'm just happy to get off the streets at the moment. The desperation out there is paranormal. (*Having settled herself, she sits up.*) You wanna fuck me or anything, Eddie, before I go to sleep?

EDDIE (*pacing toward the kitchen, he stops, looks at her*): No.

DONNA: Great. (*Lying down, preparing for sleep.*) Not that I don't want to, I'm just sleepy.

EDDIE: You want a lude, or anything?

DONNA: No.

EDDIE: Valium? (*Upstage, he leans against the landing, his arms hooked on the railing as he looks at her.*)

DONNA: No. 'Night.

EDDIE: Good night.

DONNA: Pleasant dreams.
  (*The harmonica theme begins: lyrical, yearning. DONNA lies on the couch, going to sleep. The lights narrow to hold only DONNA on the couch and EDDIE by the landing. Then the lights fade quickly out, as the music plays on, the last lyrics of "Unchained Melody" coming on in the dark.*)

CURTAIN

AFTERWORD

by David Rabe

The fact that I write a play with only the slightest premeditation regarding its intentions and implications, and then come through the simple passage of time along with the process of rehearsal and study to an intense and extensive understanding of the completed play's subterranean nature and needs, and that I am then devoted to the expression of these themes with a fanatical ardor, is a continual experience of amazement for me.

I remember beginning *Hurlyburly* with an impulse that took its shape, at least partly, in a mix of feelings spawned in my own experiences and also from my observations of the prices some men were paying from within their varied armored and defended stances—the current disorientation and accompanying anger many feel at having been flung out from the haven of their sexual and marital contexts and preconceptions. Whether they were right or wrong was not at all my concern, but the fact that they had been raised in a certain manner with certain obligations, duties and expectations (all defined as natural) which, though they led to privilege in the social order, carried with them certain hidden but equally inevitable effects of personal and emotional self-distortion, a crippling. Around me, and within myself, I felt I saw the wild reactions of creatures who had been recently given the good news that they had brutalized large portions of themselves for a disreputable cause, and now, if only they would quickly change, they would find fulfillment. Trained to control their feelings and think, they must now stop thinking and feel. Having been trained to be determined, hard, and dominant, they must now swoon into the ecstasies of submission. It was a confusing melee of contradictory exhortations, a great many of which, both past and present, came from women. On one hand these men had the admonitions and codes of their childhoods, while on the other there were their companions and contemporaries, who, awakened by the Women's Liberation Movement, were now pointing angrily to claim obvious rights for which they had, to all appearances in the past, lacked all desire. In this disturbing crunch of righteously contradictory commands, a great many men simply recoiled or, suspecting a further treachery, grew mean and wary or ossified defiantly, or felt that without their gains they would vanish, or simply loved their privilege more than what they had lost, or experienced their losses as gains. And some of all of these, along with others who had in fact attempted the change but ended up stranded, were sustaining themselves with a wide variety of drugs, or spinning out into brief but costly episodes of self-destructive frenzy, or even dropping dead. Not that I felt that the provocations of purely sociological change were the exclusive substance of their fates, but this was what I knew at this point which was, as I have stated, my crude and preliminary beginning.

A second factor in the brew was an impulse to venture near at least the appearances of the so-called "realistic" or "well-made" play, which in my view is that form which thinks that cause and effect are proportionate and clearly apparent, that people know what they are doing as they do it, and that others react accordingly, that one thing leads to another in a rational, mechanical way, a kind of Newtonian clock of a play, a kind of Darwinian assemblage of detail which would then determine the details that must follow, the substitution of the devices of logic for the powerful sweeps of pattern and energy that is our lives.

To start, I merely started: I wrote whatever I could, any scene or exchange of dialogue that occurred to me with no concern for sequence, hoping only for vitality, and believing I would find within the things I wrote the cues for order. I remember having written much of Act One, and perhaps two thirds of Act Two—enough to know that Phil would die—and then I found myself at the beginning of the last scene, the return from Phil's funeral, and suddenly the dialogue pertaining to the note and anagram began to show up.

I remember being baffled and thrilled. The content of the note, "The guy who dies in an accident understands the nature of destiny," was in no way preplanned, and I had no idea what the dictionary would offer by way of illumination until, like Eddie, I went to it. What it gave, which is what is quoted in the play, made for me an eerie and comforting sense, however enigmatic it might appear: "If you die in a happening that is not expected, foreseen or intended, you understand the inevitable or necessary succession of events." With this discovery, which was itself an outcome of chance, the play took on an entrancing addition.

And so it proceeded: I recollect early days in rehearsal when questions were addressed to me and I had no answers. I had no knowledge as to what a character was up to or intended, or what a scene was meant to convey, and I was forced to answer from this not-knowing. And yet I had to note that as moments were worked on or characters' motives or states attempted or discussed, I would have a strong sense of what was not correct, and occasionally, as time went on and our process took us to Chicago, I began to possess a certainty or two about what a character was or wanted as opposed to merely knowing what he wasn't or what it was he didn't want.

In the beginning we all had felt that the aspects of the play which would prove difficult to contend with in rehearsal would be the male characters' feelings about the female characters, and the actors' and actresses' encounters with these feelings. However, as rehearsal progressed, what we found was that the women came in and did their work rather simply and directly and the development of their scenes progressed rather quickly. Meanwhile, the men were bickering and struggling with feelings of competitiveness and resentment, shifting alliances, hurt feelings, and a fear that the play was going to crush us all collectively and individually. In other words, the difficulty in the play was in what the men wanted from and dreaded in one another: who was boss and could anybody be trusted? Somewhere in the encounter with this experience I began to see that, certainly, there were sociological considerations in the play—evaluations of the relationships between men and women in a specific time, and a specific place (though I personally feel the Hollywood connection has been vastly over-emphasized in reactions to the play, and that this is a tactic for pushing the implications of it into some quarantined region or eccentricity—"the West Coast"—so that it need not be considered as personally pertinent). Yet beyond these contemporary observations some other set of forces was at work, and in the deeper architecture of the play the women were the thrusts of emotion, the threatening surges of the forces of feeling, as if the play were one huge personality at war with itself, filled with dread of feeling on one hand and a sense somewhere in its guts that to be in charge was only an illusion of safety, that control was in fact the enterprise of hanging mid-air in the unbuoyed substanceless claims of ego.

It was at this point that I encountered in a book I had owned for years but left unread a passage offering a Jungian interpretation of a New Testament parable:

The King is the central authority, a symbol of the Self. He identifies himself with "the least"—that aspect of the personality which is despised and is considered to have no value. "The least" is hungry and thirsty; that is, it is the needy, desirous side of ourselves. It is a stranger, referring to that aspect which is lonely and unaccepted. It is naked, that is, exposed and unprotected. It is sick, the side of the psyche that is diseased, pathological, neurotic. And finally, it is in prison—confined and punished for some transgression of collective rules and behavior. All these aspects of the rejected shadow are equated with the "King," which means psychologically that acceptance of the shadow and compassion for the inferior inner man are equivalent to acceptance of the Self.[1]

That Eddie and Mickey were the royalty in the play had been discussed, the term "princes" often used in reference to them. And Phil obviously was "the least," needy, wild, desirous, desperate, an ex-con or prisoner and mysteriously loved by Eddie—mysteriously in the sense that there could be no easily grasped rational justification for the esteem in which he was held by Eddie. Yet if this code of "King" and "least" were taken as a key for the subterranean concerns of the play then it was Eddie's affection for Phil that was, oddly enough, his highest virtue.

Days later I encountered another paragraph in the same book which stated:

"To this day God is the name by which I designate all things which cross my willful path violently and recklessly, all things which upset my subjective views, plans and intentions and change the course of my life for better or worse."

The view Jung is expressing is essentially a primitive view, albeit a conscious and sophisticated one. Jung is calling "God" what most people would call chance or accident.[2]

Certainly this would seem a correlation and validation for the apparently contradictory claims of Phil's note.

On each subsequent day as I observed rehearsals or performances in Chicago I felt my grasp of things increase, though never did I feel I reached a point of certain and complete comprehension. Then, after the New York opening, I was asked to write something for a magazine, and I found myself thinking, "All right, maybe I can. What I would like to do is to

---

[1] Edward F. Edinger, *Ego and Archetype* (New York, G. P. Putnam's Sons, 1972), p. 144.

[2] Ibid., p. 101.

make it clear—the heart of it—I'll write about the union of opposites, the alchemical theme of the play, the unconscious core."

The tone of the voice suggesting this tactic was quite angry, I remember, bitter and rebellious for it felt the reception of the play to date had been without any attention to such undertones. Yet I did nothing, and felt I would probably do nothing, until one night I received a phone call from a friend who, having seen the play in both Chicago and New York, wanted to tell me he had read what he felt was a description of Eddie, his progress and state, in Jung's book *Mysterium Coniunctionis* in a chapter entitled, "The Conjunction," which is subtitled "The Alchemical View of the Union of Opposites."

> But if his recognition of the shadow is as complete as he can make it, then conflict and disorientation ensue, an equally strong Yes and No which he can no longer keep apart by a rational decision. *He cannot transform his clinical neurosis into the less conspicuous neurosis of cynicism;* in other words, he can no longer hide the conflict behind a mask. It requires a real solution and necessitates a third thing in which the opposites can unite. Here the logic of the intellect usually fails, for in a logical antithesis there can be no third. The "solvent" can only be of an irrational nature. In nature the resolution of opposites is always an energetic process: she acts symbolically in the truest sense of the word, doing something that expresses both sides, just as a waterfall visibly mediates between above and below.[3] (Emphasis added.)

Excited by a sense of relevance, I glanced about at the nearby paragraphs and noted almost immediately something in the preceding lines:

> Such a situation is bound to arise when the analysis of the psychic contents, of the patient's attitude and particularly of his dreams, has brought the compensatory or complementary im-

[3] C. J. Jung, *Mysterium Coniunctionis*, trans. by R. F. C. Hill (Princeton, A Bollingen Series, 1963), p. 495.

ages from the unconscious so insistently before his mind that the conflict between the conscious and the unconscious personality becomes open and critical. When this confrontation is confined to partial aspects of the unconscious the conflict is limited and the solution simple: *the patient, with insight and some resignation or a feeling of resentment, places himself on the side of reason and convention.* Though the unconscious motifs are repressed again, as before, the unconscious is satisfied to a certain extent, because the patient must now make a conscious effort to live according to its principles and, *in addition, is constantly reminded of the existence of the repressed by annoying resentments.*[4] (Emphasis added.)

For me, then, exposure to the entirety of this quote along with the others I had encountered produced a capacity in me to speculate confidently on the dynamics at the base of the play: there was Mickey, a figure apparently settled on the side of convention and reason, yet full of resentment and animosity, however veiled, against Phil, who was the shadow, the prisoner, the outlaw, the ex-con of banished passions, while it was Eddie who had been carried to a recognition of "Phil" from which he could not retreat, the "Phil" in himself, the forces of vitality and disorder with which Phil was identified and to which Eddie was now drawn with an equally strong Yes and No that he could no longer control and manipulate through rational decision nor could he in the end maintain his masks as Mickey could, nor any longer find comfort in the consolations of cynicism offered by Mickey. Though Eddie might try to aid Phil to learn to control and understand himself, Mickey would ridicule the effort, seeking at every opportunity to mock or provoke Phil. And, in addition, it had to be recognized that, however much Eddie might base his relationship with Phil on a real enjoyment and love, it was also founded, at least partly if not equally, upon the belief that Phil and the powers in his realm must be channeled or they would overwhelm large and essential quantities of what

[4] Ibid., p. 494.

Eddie thought to be himself. Where Mickey might oppose the threat of Phil with the simple tactic of rational condemnation and, by this means, keep himself well removed from any possible influence, Eddie, no longer capable of maintaining such a purely cerebral stance, was drawn toward the dangers of conflict and disorientation as if spellbound. And in this play it was the women who were most familiar with this state, and finally its fullest embodiment, for they were clearly more intimate with the spectrum of their emotional life, and lacking social station, they were to a large extent without conventional power. Yet they had their effect. For though they were brought in again and again as coins to be passed among the men, in exchanges in which it was expected of them that they would serve as pacifiers to discharge some male's high state of stress or emotion, it is certainly true that, more often than not, they confounded this function, tending quite powerfully to arouse in the men the very thing they had been brought in to diminish—a more extreme state of disruptive emotion. The immensity of the effort of the men to diminish and trivialize, categorize, and imprison the force they felt to be in the women was a measure of the fear they had of the chaos they felt to reside there—though it no doubt resided at least equally, if not predominantly within themselves, then "Phil."

Somewhere in the midst of these considerations I recollected a statement I had made quite early in rehearsal when, in an effort to articulate what the overall pattern of the play was, I said that it was the story of how "Eddie, through the death of Phil, was saved from being Mickey." Clearly it seemed to me that, though I had been unable at that point to delineate the steps by which this pattern progressed, I had been correct in what instinct had conceived for me. Perhaps now I hoped I might be able to uncover the exact way this theme was the essence of the play itself.

Intending to publish in this afterword what I might discover, I wrote pages and pages on the various relationships within the play, but in the end decided that their publication would be inadvisable. General thematic guidelines might be fairly suggested, but to attempt detailed instructions would be, I felt, an intrusive mistake, however much these instructions might have impressed me as appropriate.

Also, I had come in the aftermath of the production to feel that much of what we had excised from the original text had not been cut merely to contend with undue length but to alter meaning and invent intent. Though I had addressed this issue in the published text I nevertheless found that, because I had been provoked, much of what I was writing to the purpose of interpretation was in fact rebuttal, and because it was rebuttal, it was symbiotically connected to that which it challenged and to this extent, which was large, it was not free. With this realization I ended all thought of any step-by-step analysis for publication, and considered seriously, and with some relief, the complete abandonment of the idea of this afterword.

Yet the briefest contemplation of this decision put me face to face with my desire to make available to any interested reader the quotes I had found which had so intrigued me. To simply place them at the front of the book would run inescapably the risk of creating the impression that I had read them and then written the play according to their directions, which would not be merely a mistaken impression, but a hugely mistaken impression. For I knew without a doubt that had I read them prior to having written the play, I would not have understood them, let alone been capable of creating some dramatic, schematic demonstration of them.

And so, out of these varied circumstances and impulses, was fashioned this rather peculiar, though from my vantage point enjoyable, essay. The reader may take it as he pleases, which of course is something he hardly needs my permission or encouragement to do.

What I do feel justified, if not even obligated, to declare, however, is my sense that the play is its own expression, and by this I mean it has no "mouthpiece" character. No one in it knows what it is about. It has no character who is its spokesman. Not Eddie, and certainly not Mickey. Though it might be said that the play finally makes itself manifest through Eddie, he is not its embodiment, and he does not understand it.

Because in the end the essential core of the thing is in "accidents" and "destiny" and the idea that in some way they are the same thing. For, in all honesty, who among us would have devised the life he is living, however good or bad it might be at any given moment, when it must have its ultimate, inescapable and unforeseeable end? Were we not, I thought, all making do with what we had been given, and taking credit for having accomplished far more than we had in fact determined? Because always under the little we could will and then attain there was some unknown immensity on which we stood and all utterly beyond us. As the simplest and most obvious example, is not each heartbeat again and again beyond our control? Who would ever will for himself any death or calamity? Not even the suicide in fact wills "death." For a person cannot will an event of which he is utterly ignorant. The cessation of life is not death. The willful cessation takes us into something about which we know nothing, definitively, however educated our guess, however confident our logic. At the stopping of life there will be an unknown something or nothing at all, and neither is anything with which we can claim familiarity, or over which we can claim dominion. And if the bad or undesirable was then so clearly beyond our reach, on the basis of what grandiose system of self-deception did we take credit for the good?

In other words, not only did the play have no "spokesman," but it progressed on the basis of its theme—that out of apparent accidents is hewn destiny. It consisted of scenes in which no character understood correctly the nature of the events in which he was involved, nor did anyone perceive "correctly" their consequences. Beat by beat, then, the play progressed with each character certain about the point of the event in which he was involved, and no two characters possessing the same certainty, while beneath these abundant and conflicting personal conceptions was the event whose occurrence moved them on to what would follow, where they would each be confidently mistaken again.

Finally, a word on the title. When the play was in notes, which consisted of nothing more than the first line or two, it was called "Guy's Play." When I had finished it I had a long list of titles, none of which seemed quite appropriate.

Then one day while the play was in rehearsal I was looking at a piece of prose I had been working on in which the word "hurlyburly" occurred, and I thought, "That could be it." Still, as rehearsal progressed, there was vacillation on my part regarding the title, and there was encouragement from others regarding this vacillation. Then one morning, I awoke to find myself thinking that I should look in *Macbeth* and I would find justification for the title there. I opened my favorite copy, an old maroon edition, one volume of a set that was given to me by my father and mother, having been given to them by my Dad's mother, and there it was in the first four lines, "When the hurlyburly's done, When the battle's lost and won." Certainly I had read *Macbeth* before, and certainly I knew that the word was "Shakespearean," but until that moment I had no conscious knowledge that the word was in *Macbeth* and in the first four lines. This was for me sufficient validation, however, and it became the title and almost a lot more. For as I was readying the text for publication, and fooling with quotes of one kind or another which I might include, it occurred to me that the three acts could be titled by the first lines from *Macbeth*. I had felt for a long time that the play was in many ways a trilogy, each act an entity, a self-contained action however enhanced it might be by the contents of the other acts and the reflections that might be sent back and forth between all three. So for a time I considered naming the three acts, "When Shall We Three Meet Again?", "In Thunder, Lightning or in Rain?" and "When the Hurlyburly's Done, When the Battle's Lost and Won," but in the end decided against it.

Neither the text nor the stage directions in this volume

reflect the original Broadway staging. My exploration of the play has continued through several other productions and a great deal of thought and study of the text as I reconstructed it for publication. Finally, in the fall of 1988, I directed a production at the Westwood Playhouse in Los Angeles, California. This present text is based on that production in both stage directions and dialogue.